SPIRITUAL SPRING

Journey to Self-Love

Ruby Rose Taylor

© 2020 Ruby Rose Taylor

Ruby Rose Taylor has asserted her right to be identified as the author of this work in accordance with the Copyright, Designs and Patents Act 1988. All rights reserved. No part of this book may be reproduced by any mechanical, photographic or electronic process, or in the form of a phonographic recording, nor may it be stored in a retrieval system, transmitted, or otherwise be copied for public or private use – other than for "fair use" as brief quotations embodied in articles and reviews without prior written permission of the publisher.

The author of this book does not dispense medical advice nor prescribe the use of any technique as a form of treatment for physical or medical problems without the advice of a physician, either directly or indirectly. The intent of the author is only to offer information of a general nature to help you in your quest for physical, emotional, mental and spiritual fitness and good health. The author assumes no responsibility for your actions.

ISBN: 978-06486835-5-1
Edited by: Carol Campbell

CONTENTS

Prologue A BLISSFUL JOURNEY v
Chapter 1 FAIRY TALES 9
Chapter 2 LIFE 17
Chapter 3 THE PROGRAM 25
Chapter 4 SELF-LOVE 35
Chapter 5 FLASHBACK 41
Chapter 6 BIRTH 47
Chapter 7 FREEDOM 59
Chapter 8 MIND MASTERY 67
Chapter 9 CHILDHOOD BELIEFS 81
Chapter 10 A TEST 87
Chapter 11 BUYING HAPPINESS 95
Chapter 12 ALTERING STATES 99
Chapter 13 DISCOVERING DREAMS 109
Chapter 14 CREATION CEREMONY 117
Chapter 15 HAPPY HEART 129
Chapter 16 ROSES OF LOVE 135
Chapter 17 CHANGING TIDES 143
Chapter 18 SOARING SPIRIT 151
Chapter 19 RE-BIRTH 163
Epilogue DEVINE HILL 167
ABOUT THE AUTHOR 171
ACKNOWLEDGEMENTS 173

*In memory of my cousin, Olivia.
May self-love heal us all.*

Dedicated to Guy

Prologue

A BLISSFUL JOURNEY

Making my way in a spiral direction through the beautiful trees, plants and flowers I reach Devine Hill. Overlooking the small township of Ocean Shores, I am at the top of a glorious hill, greeted by golden hues. The glimmer of the rising sun warms me, as I experience the majesty of Lion's Lookout.

Sitting down in awe on the memorial bench, I notice a dedication to a poet who was loved and lost. With a straight spine I sit on the bench and face the sun, I close my eyes and I hold the body of my guitar close to my heart. I caress its soft strings and I gently pluck a melody that compliments the sound of the ocean. The birds are my back up choir and a cool breeze blows through my tangerine hair as I surrender into nothingness.

I inhale the fresh air and I feel grateful for my simple life. I look toward the heavens and I bow my head to my heart in reverence to my almighty Creator. I feel blessed to be following my heart and learning to trust the divine in all things. I am learning to trust and my new journey living like this has sent me away from the confines of the classroom walls, far from the busy beat of Brisbane's hectic streets and straight into the heart of nature.

Staring into the crystal blue water, the sandy white coastline is an iconic emblem of Australia's stunning landscape. A well-known Australian singer; John Williamson comes to my mind, as his song: "True Blue" plays in my memory.

"True blue Australia." I hear myself say. My eyes drift across the picturesque beaches and stop at an outcropping of rocks, cradling a prominent lighthouse in the distance. The lighthouse is a popular destination twenty minutes south of Ocean Shores, in a town called Byron Bay.

As the cloudy blue heavens draw my focus closer and my mind begins to expand, I start to feel the divine presence of inspiration working through me. Pulses of energy at the crown of my head awaken and a surge of light enters my being. I surrender into complete presence and I begin to play chords and sing a stream of channelled words.

"Great Creator, your light shines to me from the heavens, like a beacon through the clouds. Your light shines to me like the sun setting over the ocean. Your light fills my soul and fills my whole.

Great Creator of all that is, you know in the hearts of all souls on this planet Earth, you know their every thought, their every fear and I'm asking you, what do I say now, what do I tell them?" The Great Creator answered through my song,

"Look up, all you teachers. Look up and pray to the heavens above. Look up, all seekers and you will find your way. The madness is going away. Look to the light of the sky, look to the light in your eyes. Look to the light and you will see. You will know your truth. Look to the formations in your mind that arise with the light and you will rise with the light. You are one, you are the same, you are love, you will always be this way. There is nothing to fear, but the fear of fear. Claim."

"Claim?" I sang.

"Claim your birthright, feel the light in the night and you will shine. Yes, you will shine. When all has come and gone, you will know once again, because you will be home.

You were sent here for a mission - to be more than you can be in this life. So, you've got to give it up. You've got to give it all up. You've got to let it die. You've got to let it all die, to know what you are capable of.

Take it higher, take your love and bring it to the sky up above. Take it higher, take your love, bring it up. Higher and higher. Soaring high above your mind, higher you will find your highest self. Don't stray down too long. You need to raise your eyes high, so you can passage through this time.

You've got to find yourself on a journey. Put yourself on a journey to love. You've got to be on a journey. Life isn't all that you think it is, when you're waiting, when you're anticipating and losing time over things, you're losing life, you're losing time. Take yourself back to the moment. Back to the now, back to the sun, where you can create.

You can create. You've got to get your thoughts on their way. Your thoughts are taking you away. Steer them down. Steer them down to Mother Earth. Bring them down to your soul. Bring them down to the holy land. Bring your heart up. Bring your heart up, up, up. Bring your mind up into the sun. Let the light shine through and shine, shine, shine."

"Wow! I shouted to the heavens.

"I feel enlivened! Thank you! What a divine message for humanity right now!" The Creator's transmission was flowing though me and I knew I was experiencing the divine. Feelings of gratitude surged through me, and I remembered how lucky I was to have developed such a close connection to the divine. It hadn't always been the case though, until I discovered how to love myself.

Chapter 1

FAIRY TALES

The three ugly step-sisters seized me, dragged me by the hair and threw me into a room.

"Wake up and smell the roses, Ruby Rose! Stop daydreaming! This is where you'll stay until you face the truth!" I pleaded with them.

"One choice! That's all it was. One bad, life-changing decision. Please don't leave me here. I want to go back to the way my life was before!"

They ignored me and slammed the door, leaving me in darkness.

I sobbed to myself, as I leant up against the back wall. I could hear my wicked stepmother announcing my predicament loud and clear.

"This is not a rehearsal, Ruby Rose. You're not an actor on stage; this is your life. Don't slip out of reality. You made the choice; now you're going to have to pay the price."

Disbelief numbed my entire body as I struggled to come to terms with the direction my life had taken. I had no choice but to face the pending destination. My hands gripped my face and I desperately attempted to cover my eyes and block out the truth of who I was. I couldn't face the coming surgery and I couldn't believe where I was. How did I end up here? Where was he when I needed him? I'd heard people say they'd move mountains for love. This can't be love; this feels nothing like love!

If I could find a single thread of logic. Anything to bring me back to reality. Some evidence or rational reasoning that might explain why this happened, maybe then I would feel better.

There had to be an answer. There is always meaning behind everything, but as much as I desperately wanted to find something to cling to, all I could feel was pain. As I moved my hands down from my face and to my stomach, I could feel the remnants and fragments of death still lingering within me.

The guilt enveloped me further and I succumbed to the deep despair resonating within the violated womb inside me. As I spiralled deeper into the black heart of my terrifying abyss, I knew I was a murderer. The evidence was clear. The cold hard facts were that Sam had never really loved me. He may have said it, but his actions spoke the sad, sad truth.

The doctors and nurses huddled around me in a professional manner. They were offering me reassuring smiles of compassion and understanding as they checked my blood pressure and prepared the gas for the coming procedure. Hopefully this time I would wake up, and it would all be over. Hopefully this time the abortion would be complete.

"How are you feeling?" One nurse asked me politely. I looked at her almost on the brink of a breakdown. Was I supposed to act like I was okay? Was I supposed to robustly reply,

"Yeah, great thanks! It meant nothing to me that a life was growing inside me and that I opted for two pills to take my baby away. It meant nothing that I went through three days of bleeding and agony alone. It meant nothing to me that it didn't even work properly and now I am in hospital about to undergo my second abortion in a week.

"Yeah, everything's perfect. It couldn't be better and, how are you? How's your life lately? Any surprising twists of fate?"

In complete resignation, I fell backwards into a sea of pristine, white sheets.

"Yeah, I'm okay thanks." I replied weakly, hoping the sheets would swallow me up so I could disappear down the sinking sands of my life. I felt stained, dirty and ashamed. I felt far from clean and a long way from Doreen Virtue's angel cards that Sam had given me as an early birthday present the night, I broke the news to him. He was being thoughtful and kind, and it had made it even harder to tell him that I was pregnant.

"Thank you so much, Sam! What are they?"

"They're just a bit of fun." he'd said shyly.

Out of curiosity, I'd drawn one of the cards and almost dropped it in shock, as the image of an angel protecting the pregnant belly of a woman said: Congratulations on the birth of this new period of your life. I stared at it in shock. How was it possible? How could the card be so accurate? I tried to maintain my poker face; I didn't want to break the news to Sam until we were outside the pub. But I was unnerved by the card's message. Unfortunately, while the angels might have been happy for me about this new period of my life, I certainly wasn't and, when I finally plucked up the courage to tell Sam the news, it didn't go down well. I could still hear Sam's words,

"If you go ahead and have this baby, what's this going to mean for you and your family? They don't need the added pressure; and what will my family think of me? What is Jane going to do? You know what she'll do, Ruby Rose. She'll take my unborn baby and I'll never see him again. She will never speak to me after this and my family will disown me."

The colour in Sam's face was draining fast, now ashen. I could see his mind was filled with dread as he imagined the way his life was about to unravel.

Sam had wanted a simple solution to the problem. He'd wanted it kept quiet and he'd wanted it to go away. So that's what I did; I made it all go away. Well, that was the way it was supposed to happen. Nice and easy, but I wasn't getting off lightly. There were significant repercussions for me and my oral abortion.

"Yes, okay, I'll have an abortion," I said, wanting to ease his anxiety and make it all better for him.

"I'll call the clinic tomorrow and make an appointment. I'll do it before I leave for Bali."

"You're the best! You're the three Rs, babe! You are rational, reasonable and reliable.

"But Sam, what about the baby's soul?"

"Don't worry about that! You grow a soul; it's too early for that. There's nothing to worry about, everything will be fine!"

After he intelligently minimised all my Christian concerns, I said: "I'll do whatever's best for you, Sam. I hadn't spoken to you when I decided to have our baby, and I was prepared to deal with it by myself. I didn't realise it was going to affect your life so much. I want this to be a decision we make together."

"I want you to have an abortion."

"Okay, fine but ... I'm really scared that if I go through with this ... I'll end up resenting you ... I may even hate you for it."

He hugged me and together we wept. For Sam, that was a risk he was all too willing to take. Squeezing my eyes shut to stop the emotion flowing, I tried to block out the memories. His face flashed towards me as doctors, nurses and operating staff began wheeling me into theatre. The hospital lights darkened, and a whistling wind howled loudly in my soul. I was alone. He wasn't coming, and I was being expected to pick up the pieces of my bleeding womb and carry on. After I'd messaged him to say that something wasn't right and I was being admitted to hospital, he'd written back.

"Keep me posted."

Not a phone call to check in and see how I was going but an impersonal text message with no tone. I'd practically screamed in rage when he made no mention of coming to see me. I was instantly filled with bitterness.

"Can you hear the tone in my voice now, Sam? This is going to be the second attempt of our shameful abortion. Do you know what I've been through?"

The nurse and the doctors asked me: "Is there anyone you would like us to call?"

"Yes, a guy actually. His name is Sam. He's currently hosting a baby shower for his unborn son. Can you put Jane on? There's something I want to tell her. Tell her the "nice" girl protecting the truth for him is on the phone. The reasonable, reliable and rational one!"

I sighed.

Chapter 1: Fairy Tales

"No, there's no-one to call." Tears welled up as the hospital staff exchanged looks. I turned on to my side, moving away from their inquisitive faces. I thought about the people I could call. I had already spoken to my sister and a friend from work. I could have called more family and friends for support, but I was dull and void. I was worthless and completely damaged goods. I was in pain; I was in anguish and I was completely lost.

Inner desolation began to suffocate me inside a barren landscape of dead air. Listlessness consumed my entire being, filling me with queasy unease. I felt like a dead corpse, devoid of all life. Get me out of here. What is this place? This is not my life! When was this written in my dreams and how is this the "happy ever after" Cinderella story I believed in?

"I fucking believed your fairy tales. Fuck you Disney!"

I grabbed my rose-coloured glasses covering my eyes. "Third time lucky, hey Ruby Rose. Another bubble of love disastrously popping again!"

"Great track record you've got going with men, you loser!"

I thrashed in anger as I threw my glasses across the room, smashing them in the process. Laughing deliriously, I watched as broken shards ricocheted off the white walls. Was this an asylum? Was I losing my mind? Razor blades of lightning slashed the sheets and great cracks of thunder split my heart open. My heart lay in three bloody pieces and was pumping blood across my bed.

The gas mask floated above me and I could see dainty fingers gripping the edges of my mask. The nurse carefully placed it over my mouth and nostrils. I breathed in deeply, welcoming the sweet relief from my stressful reality. All the pain and distress began to float away. I was feeling light and fuzzy. I was fading into nothingness far, far away.

"Take me away and don't ever wake me up," I mumbled to the nurse as I felt myself slipping down inside a vessel that was taking me to a far and distant place. Scenes of my life began screening inside the vessel walls; it was as if I were watching a horror film. The worst week of my life began projecting onto a big screen inside the vessel

I was floating inside. I was descending deeper and deeper, and it was getting darker the deeper I was going.

Bubbles began to escape from my diving mask, as I watched the images being screened across the wall. I watched myself holding onto Sam's sweaty hand in the abortion clinic. My autograph flashed up and I studied my signature closely as I gave written consent to terminate the life within me.

"No don't do it! Stop! Ruby Rose, stop! You'll regret it! Don't sacrifice yourself for him. He's not worth it; he only cares about himself."

I began to scream, as my mask filled with water. I watched in sadness as the doctor pointed out the early stages of life on the ultrasound. I could hear the heartbeat echoing around the vessel as if it were cinema surround sound. I put my hands around my ears to block out the sounds of life, as I watched on fearfully. Oh no, this is my life-changing moment. Do I really have to see this again? I watched as I swallowed the oral medication to abort the life growing inside me.

I felt myself thrash in the water helplessly. I was screaming at the images, but I was completely powerless to change the events that were now set in stone. The days moved forward on a photographic time lapse and I was digging a shallow grave. I was making a small hole beneath my aloe vera plants and burying the miscarried matter I'd terminated. I watched as heartfelt, loving messages between Sam and I typed themselves onto the projected screen, revealing a loving conversation we had shared.

"I love you, Ruby. If things were different, I would have supported you to have our baby."

Tears streamed down my face. In the next image, I was walking the streets alone. I was clutching my stomach and kneeling in pain beside a drain on the pavement. I watched myself bravely trying to remain calm, despite the uncertainty of my symptoms. Then, my friend and I were at lunch and I'd barely been able to eat. I was doubled over the table in pain, holding my stomach, as I explained to her that I needed some painkillers. She'd taken me to the hospital, and I watched as my friend waved goodbye leaving me there.

"Flash, flash, flash." The projection was suddenly losing power. All my memories were flashing past as the final fragments of my projected consciousness revealed Sam and I sitting at a coffee table over the road from the abortion clinic right before I swallowed those life-changing pills. He was talking and I was listening. He was complaining and I was nodding submissively and offering him empathy.

"My boss was so annoying today when I told her I needed to go to some appointments for my back. She was really on my case about it."

I walked up to the live projection in front of me and I pushed myself out of the way. I slapped him hard in the face with the truth of who he really was.

"That's because you're a liar! How can you find it so easy to lie? I hate you; you're the scum of the earth! Can't you face the cold, hard facts? You're a rat! A dirty cover-up. Women know! We always know! Deep down, we feel it. Bit by bit, we lose our sense of self, because of men like you ... men like you are cowards." I softened a little now,

"But then again, Sam, to be fair, I guess you didn't think it could get any worse, did you? You probably didn't imagine that it could get any more complicated than it already was. First with Jane and the unwanted pregnancy. Then you weren't banking on a second pregnancy, were you? I bet that caught you off-guard. Classic fairy-tale start isn't it? Just fucking perfect!"

The lights flashed and dimmed across the projection. The image of Sam disappeared, and darkness filled the strange vessel. I began searching frantically for the control buttons. There was no light and I was suddenly frightened.

"Where the hell was I? What is this place? How do I get out of here? Somebody? Anybody? Please help me."

A thousand voices in my head were screaming in terror as the walls were closing in around me. The stench of my desperation mingled with my morning perfume and my body odour was now completely stale. I reeked of trepidation. Time began dripping with sweat and my face was pale with fear. The whites around my eyes were expanding as my pupils dilated furiously. I fumbled around in the dark, consumed by fear barely breathing shallow gulps of air. I ran my anxious hands across what felt like controls. What was that? I could feel something ... yes, it felt like a button. I pressed it and it lit up. Like magic, the doors opened.

Chapter 2

LIFE

Wow! Amazed by the sudden change, I felt a rush around my feet as water gushed out of the vessel and spilt out of the opening.

Where am I now? Looking down at my bare feet, I could see the sunlight touching my toes as sunshine poured into the vessel. I stepped forward. The soles of my feet were walking on soft, green grass, and my eyes widened as I saw a beautiful garden that looked like a Monet painting. Every detail was an elegant brush stroke of vibrant colour. Bright-pink tulips, yellow daffodils, purple irises and a sprinkling of blue forget-me-nots were flourishing in an abundant bounty of spring throughout the garden. It was both dreamy and inviting.

As my eyes adjusted to the splendour, I noticed a crystal-clear lake, surrounded by tall willow trees, weeping gently into the water. Vivid greenery was being illuminated by the sun's rays, as vibrant green hues shone through the leafy canopy and sparkles of light landed gently on lily-pads. The lily-pads moved with the gentle breeze, innocently drifting along the water's edge. Lotus flowers adorned the mirrored reflection in perfect patterns of pink and green and, as I stared more closely, I could see a sleeping horse with wings floating on the surface of the water.

"Pegasus? On the lake? What is this place?"

I spoke quietly and saw Pegasus opening his eyes. Kneeling on the ground, I picked up a nearby stone and threw it as far as I could. As I did, flying doves crossed the sky in an arc. The stone landed in the centre of the lake with a loud and pronounced, plop! Circular ripples moved outwardly across the water. As the waking animal stood up and began to move, its wings began circling as it prepared to fly. I watched in awe as the majestic horse flew from the lake into the sky. Tiny droplets showered the lake as the beautiful animal disappeared in the blue heavens.

I turned in a daze at the magic of my surroundings. Little white rabbits were nibbling quietly on the grass and their floppy ears were raised curiously toward the sky. They watched me carefully. Blue wrens hopped and sang as they gathered sticks for their nest. Baby joeys were tucked comfortably in their mother's pouches and they peered out at me with innocent eyes.

"Where am I?" I thought, as I breathed more freely. The sweet relaxation of the sun's bliss was incredible. I gently smiled. It felt good to smile again – really, good.

My eyes widened with surprise as I noticed sparkles of light shining on all the plants in the garden. I saw a group of butterflies dancing in time to a rhythm being created by the shimmering sun. Crotchets, quavers and other musical notes hovered up and down on an invisible score of music. They were all dancing in time with the butterflies. One of the butterflies began flying towards me.

Transfixed, I stared at its emerald and gold wings. It was moving gracefully to me. Captivated by its beauty, I looked closely and noticed its blue eyes were serenading me with kindness and love.

"Ruby Rose, come over here!"

A tall, slender woman called to me. She raised her hand and waved. She smiled brightly and her fine, curly, red hair had the vibrancy of gold.

"Hello?" I didn't know what to say but moved curiously towards her.

"Look at me." She laughed playfully as she spun around like a ballerina and danced to the music. Her body was toned and athletic, and she had a sparkle about her as though she was a magical fairy.

"What do you notice about me?" she asked enthusiastically with wide eyes.

In that moment the penny dropped.

"Oh, my goodness. You're me!" I exclaimed.

She was stunning. Everything about her said "I am beautiful, and I am worthy". She was radiant and glowing. Her skin was incredible, and her body was feminine and alluring. I looked at her with a downward glance, sheepishly ashamed at my dishevelled appearance. I was feeling self-conscious because I was wearing an unattractive, oversized hospital gown. She couldn't be me. How was that possible? I felt my head drop in embarrassment and my cheeks turn bright red.

"Know your power and bring it forth," she said. "I am you. Look at me and begin to remember who you are. You are me, and I am who you will become if you choose self-love. I want you to experience a life worth living so step up, stand up and raise your head with confidence."

I did as she commanded. I stood tall and instantly felt more powerful. This woman demanded respect and I certainly didn't want to offend her.

"Good. Now open your eyes." Her eyes burnt with focused intensity into mine. Bluish-grey irises, with flecks of gold stared straight into the deepest part of me. She was magnetic, and I could feel it.

"Stand in the light. Do not be afraid. We do not have much time and there are many things I must tell you. Listen closely to what I have to say. These are the words of your truth.

"I know you have been searching, seeking, and looking for the meaning in your life. You've been trying to put the pieces together, because you are hoping the puzzle will make sense, but there are still many pieces missing and that is why you are here. I will help you see the picture more clearly. I know you're desperate to understand your recent heartbreak and that you're searching for true love. You are on the right path. It is only in seeking that you shall find true love.

"There have been many times in your life when you've been on an adventure holding an exciting treasure map in your hands. Your nature is to be very curious. You are willing to test your limits and challenge yourself. Normally, you have a free spirit but lately you've begun to feel that your life is fraught with peril and disappointment. As you've approached the spots on your map that you thought were gold, you've uncovered land mines and dangerous experiences.

"You keep looking for love in all the wrong places and I cannot allow you to blow yourself up anymore. I know you're doing your best but, if you keep ignoring and repressing your deeper issues, you will keep repeating the pattern. You will need to go deeper into who you really are and face your issues head on. Are you prepared to do that?"

"Will it mean I'll find true love?"

"Absolutely, you will find the greatest love of the century."

"That sounds marvellous."

"I'd like to put you on a rapid expansion program. Are you interested in that?"

"Oh yes, please!"

"Good! Because if you make it through our program, you will enter a stage of your life called "Spiritual Spring." The old you will be your "Winter", and that part of you will break away and fall to the wayside into dust, making way for transformation, growth and enlightenment. You will blossom in all your miraculous positivity and move into a magical state of being. You will be completely alive and full of possibility.

"I have some wonderful news. Your true self is arriving, which heralds a new beginning for you."

Her words rolled around in my head. Could it really be possible that if I resolved my past and dealt with my problems then I would move into a state of Spring? What does that even mean?

"Okay," I whispered shyly. feeling uncertain and suddenly vulnerable.

"Do you want to be a lighter, brighter and happier you?"

"Yes, I desperately do."

"Well, that is what our program teaches. Come over here, Ruby Rose. Can you see the wooden table?" She pointed towards a large, smooth-surfaced table by the lake, with yellow sunflowers standing in vases."

Chapter 2: Life

"Yes, I can." I gave an affirmative nod. She was an engaging teacher and I already wanted to be a good student.

"This is a strong and sturdy table with careful craftsmanship that shows attention to detail. Notice the soft, honey colour of the oak? Can you see how it almost glows?"

"Yes."

"Look at the timber – the horizontal grain, the natural artistry of the knots – and begin to observe it more closely."

I nodded obediently and looked more intensely at the details she described.

"Do you see curious little pictures and shapes inside the natural contours of the wood?"

"Yes, I do," I said eagerly.

"Can you see a world within a world?" I looked at her, amazed. There were shapes, faces and pictures.

"Herein, lies your potential."

"My ... potential?" I quizzed her.

"On one side of the table stands a vibrant, fresh sunflower in a purple opaque vase. Can you see it?"

"Yes."

"The colour of the sunflower radiates across the garden, brightening even the shadows nearby. It's filling the garden with sunshine and strength. This represents your ability to hold light and to share your light with others. You are a leader and a goddess of love."

I looked at her with disbelief. What was she talking about? I was definitely not a goddess. On the opposite end of the table, I could see a sunflower slumped over and heavy. Its head was wilting wearily, and it was drooping from a lack of vitality.

"It does not have the strength to support itself. Can you see how the brown, curling leaves are resigned to death and decay? There is a sense of suffering. Can you feel it?"

"Yes, it feels thick and sticky," I said.

"Notice how you are compelled to pull its head up so that it's free from the struggle that's draining its face?

"Yes."

"This image represents your very existence and a way of being that has stopped working for you. A pattern you've created in your life that has trapped you in self-doubt and despair. It's time to make a choice. One way of being represents what isn't working in your life and now needs to die. The other symbolises what is available to you right now. What way of being will you choose?"

Without hesitation, I said, "The new way."

"What are you prepared to do?"

"'I'm prepared to do whatever it takes."

"This isn't the easy road. You can't flick a switch and make it magically happen. You need to be reprogrammed."

"What?"

"Don't play dumb or downplay your intelligence with me. Don't forget who you are talking to."

"Oh, yeah. Sorry, it's a bad habit."

"No, it's not a habit. It's a subconscious core belief. It needs to be reprogrammed. The question is: Are you ready? You might say you want to be free from your old ways of being, but how attached are you to your past? How willing are you to let your stories go?"

"What do you mean? Do I have to erase my past?"

"You have to be willing to start again. But, before we allow you to do that, you have to face your past."

"Oh no, I don't want to do that. Will I have any memories left?"

"You will be left with a white canvas. You will be the creator of your life. Anything you choose will be done. You will be that powerful."

I looked at her nervously, not feeling at all confident about my ability to create my life from a blank canvas. After all, I hadn't been doing too well with my life recently.

She could see the doubt on my face and said, "To be honest, I don't think you're ready. But there is an alternative if you are interested?"

"Yeah, sure."

"We can take you through one of our experiments we are currently trialling and, if you succeed, we can look at upgrading you to our program. We can discuss it then."

"What type of experiments?"

"We're calling it the Ego and Spirit Adventure. It's a new program designed to shock your system from the old way of being and wake you up."

"Wake me up?"

"Yes, we want to wake you up to a higher level of consciousness."

"How does it work?"

"It's a few levels down in the vessel that you arrived in. It's a script we're developing. There's a lot of buzz about this program. It's never been done before."

"If it's never been done before, then how can I trust it?"

"Do you understand the word 'ego'?"

"A little bit."

"Your ego is your association with your identity. This is intuitive and interactive software, designed to implement the early phase required for re-birth."

Chapter 3

THE PROGRAM

"Re-birth?"
"You heard me."
"Like a baby?
"Yes, you will be fully functional but with extras."
"Extras?"
"Yes, and there are upgrades. Using our enhancement package, you can re-enter the world knowing exactly who you are and what your mission is here on earth. But that's the final outcome.

"You're a long way away from that stage of the program. At some point in your path ahead, you may feel tempted to give up on entering "Spring" and, when that happens, try and recall the two sunflowers. You can label them as 'thriving' or 'barely surviving'. You can use them as a reminder of your two choices.

"Choice number one is your old way of being that isn't working and leaves you hurt and broken. Or you can opt for choice number two: your new way of being that makes you feel vibrantly alive and inspired.

"You seem to be obsessed with your Cinderella story and what a perfect love story should look like. We have created software to help you identify your stories and, because you've said yes to the program, you will be given teachings to help you discover your truth.

"Your ability to know and understand yourself and to question why you are the way you are, will help you to make powerful decisions as you move towards Spring.

"Just a word of warning though; you must remain mindful that as you move forward, "you" will be your biggest opponent. So be prepared. In some stages of the program we will need to test your progress towards "self-realisation", and if you give up, we will know you aren't ready."

"What will happen if I'm not ready?"

"You will need more life experiences and more lessons. It usually takes a life-changing event for people to go searching for transformation."

"No, please. I've had enough disappointments; I don't want anything else. I'm ready for this."

"We will have to wait and see. There is a lot you need to learn. My advice for you is to keep the two possibilities at the forefront of your mind. See the thriving sunflower and choose it. Acknowledge the dying one and discard it. You are always in control and you always have the choice. You can make the decision to step back from what doesn't serve you, or you can choose to live as the creator of your life. It is up to you.

"The stories you created in the early years of your life limit your greatest potential and, unfortunately, you are not alone. Many people are struggling with this, too. When you listen to your early programming as though it is your identity, you lose power around being who you really are. In all honesty, the truth is you are completely unconscious to the impact these stories are having on your life.

"Without taking the steps in our program, you won't even know they exist, or be able to understand how they even started. Consequently, you will have no power over your reactions. Your circumstances might change, but your underlying theme will always stay the same. Have you ever wondered why you keep attracting the men in your life that lie?"

"No, I've never considered it."

"Ever wondered why you attract men with addictions?"

"No... I didn't realise I was."

"That's fine. We don't expect you to have full awareness yet. You are still asleep."

"I'm still asleep?"

"Yes, but don't worry. The awakening will come and, when it does, your life will become very different to the one you have been creating unconsciously. There will come a time when you will use your awareness and manifest your future into what you truly want it to be.

"At the moment a younger, outdated version of yourself is running the show. Not only that, you've also got nasty voices of fear and doubt in your mind trying to convince you that you've wrecked your life and that you're a useless excuse for a human. Your voices tell you that you're worthless and you don't amount to anything."

She looked at me compassionately. I was struck by her depth of understanding and kindness.

"They really bring me down."

"They ... or you?"

"Me. I hear the voices and believe what they are saying."

"You're fighting against yourself when you listen to negative thoughts. You are destabilising and belittling yourself. If you don't get a handle on your mind, you will never know freedom. Your deep-seated fear is creating layer upon layer of guilt and shame. This then motivates your actions and decisions.

"Listening to the voices, stories and interpretations of fear convinces you that this is your truth. You place self-blame, criticism and judgement upon yourself and others, and you find it easier to doubt yourself than to believe in yourself. It's easier to be fearful than to trust, but what is more inviting?"

"Definitely trusting is more inviting."

"So, who exactly are you listening to and where is this source of information coming from?"

"I'm listening to the voice that says, 'I'm not lovable', 'I'm not good enough', 'I'm wrong', and 'it's all my fault'."

"Is it a credible source? How old do you think you were when you formed these beliefs?"

"I don't know."

"Take a guess."

"Ten years old?"

"No, you were five years old. In this lifetime when you formed your core beliefs, you were just an innocent child trying to make sense of the world. Can you get that, Ruby? You were an innocent child trying to make things right in your world. That's all.

"Not knowing yourself and understanding who you really are has resulted in unconscious self-sabotage and self-destruction. You must find out who you are. Otherwise, you will live your life through the distorted lens of your negative self-image, destroying all your opportunities for success."

"But how? How do I find out who I truly am? This is a question I've had for many years and I've never discovered an answer. You're my teacher, can't you tell me?"

"They need to be teaching this at school from as early as possible. Our program will help you, but you will need to be willing to do the work. It will be a very different way of looking at yourself. Are you prepared for that?"

"Yes, I am ready to look at myself in a completely new way."

"Your life purpose is to learn self-love."

"What?"

"Yes, it will change your life forever. We have the best teachers and software in this program, and we want to help you. This opportunity is given to those who are willing to do the work on themselves. It takes a very special person to get through this pathway. We believe you have what it takes to raise the vibration of the planet and awaken consciousness.

"We are investing in you, because we believe in you. You carry the light. It is within you. Don't go looking outside of yourself; the kingdom is within. She pulled out an expensive-looking camera with a lens I'd never seen before.

"Ruby Rose, this is a supernatural camera. When you look through it, all your thoughts exist in a state of perfection. The experience is quite profound because, as you are looking through this lens, you will experience enlightenment."

"Oh wow! I've always dreamed of being enlightened!"

"Dream no more because this is your reality. This is no ordinary camera and we created it specifically for the program. Every thought you experience through this viewfinder will be proactive; every idea, an opportunity; every story, a positive outcome; and every belief, limitless." She began looking through the lens. Her presence began to glow.

"What you see and feel through the camera will be your natural state without your negative beliefs, patterns or stories. Can you imagine what your life might be like without your limitations?"

"Oh, my goodness! Amazing!" I was getting excited. She placed the camera against her hip and continued explaining. Her face was alive with possibility.

"If you could experience the world through a picture-perfect lens, what would your brightest and highest thoughts be?" I thought for a minute before replying.

"Hmmm ... I am limitless and free! I am beautiful! I am at peace! I am thriving and abundant! I am lovable!"

"What thoughts and feelings give you total freedom right now?"

"I choose ... I am worthy, I am valuable, I am gifted, and I am powerful."

"Great! Now, before you hold the camera and have the ability to see and feel in picture-perfect detail, what will you choose to focus on? Your perfect relationship? Your career? Your finances? Your health and wellbeing? Your physical appearance?"

"I'd like to focus on my health and wellbeing."

"Okay, great. If you could have one perfect picture of that, what would it look like in your life?"

"I'm radiantly healthy, happy and whole! I'm complete about everything and I'm at peace with everything that has happened."

As she handed me the camera, I was instantly uplifted. I looked through the lens as she continued talking.

I was in the picture! Looking exactly as I said! Radiant, whole and complete. Light was emanating from my skin and I looked so vibrant!

"Can you get a close-up of your picture of health now? Zoom in using the top of the lens."

"Yes, I'm zooming in."

"What can you see?"

"I am alive and full of energy!"

"How do you feel?"

"I feel calm, everything is still. My thoughts aren't racing, and I am relaxed.

"What does your image of wellbeing look like?"

"I'm lying in a field of grass enjoying the glorious sunshine. I'm wearing a pretty dress and it looks like I've been making a flower crown because I look like a princess. I'm smiling, happy and free. I'm rolling down the hill like a playful child again!"

"What thoughts are you having?"

"I love life. I love everyone. The world is a special place. I am so lucky to be alive. Everything is perfect and I am loved."

"If you can feel joy looking through the camera, what is stopping you from creating your own perfect picture now?"

"Nothing."

"Exactly ... and that is what you have to do to complete the program. You need to create thoughts and feelings that master your state. We will send you challenges to test you, so practise being in a positive mindset as much as possible. You will need to prove that you can free yourself from the ferocious grip of negativity and the sharp claws of fear. We will be watching and assessing you.

"Look through the lens again and see your ideal outcome."

"My ideal outcome is to be filled with self-love."

"Great, try it out. What do you see and feel through the lens?"

"I'm seeing myself sitting by a river with my eyes closed. I'm breathing deeply, my mind is clear and it's like I'm suspended in a bubble of love."

"How about your emotions? What are you feeling?"

"I'm feeling blissful, light and uplifted. I'm very fulfilled and content. I am aware of supreme consciousness and I feel connected to everything. I can see the Creator's love in every leaf, plant and stone. I feel so loved."

"Are you beginning to notice how your thoughts create emotions? How powerful is the energy of your positive feelings?"

"My feelings are powerful. I feel great!"

I stopped looking through the lens and turned to face my teacher.

"Our program will train you to become a magnet for empowering thoughts so that you are able to treat yourself and all humans with love and respect. For you are the love in them and they are the love in you. You are one and the same."

"How is it possible that we are one and the same? I don't understand."

"That's okay; it's an advanced concept at this stage. But in time you will understand this concept. It's like acknowledging that the light in you is the same light in others; and the dark in you is the same dark in others. If you can recognise yourself in others you can connect to that sense of oneness within all beings."

"Okay, that's not so complicated."

"When you stop judging yourself and others, this proves that you are committed to loving yourself, loving others, forgiving yourself, forgiving others and accepting who you are and accepting others. Do you believe that you are doing the best you can with the situation you're in?"

I looked at her and remembered the pain of trying to do the right thing by Sam and sacrificing my own choice to have a baby just to please him. "Yes, I am doing my best."

"So, is it possible that everyone else is doing the best they can in their own personal journey, too?"

"I never thought of it like that before but, applying it to myself first, makes it so much easier to accept it in others."

"Even if another person's actions hurt you and make no sense, can you see that they are doing the best they can in the situation they're in?"

"Yes."

"Let unconditional love fill your heart now. Soften into forgiveness and release the bitter pain that is holding you hostage. Are you willing to look at Sam through this lens?"

"No! I can't do that yet. I'm sorry. I'm still angry. I'm not ready yet."

"You have a choice right now to make. You can go down this path of resistance, which is going to take you away from feeling good, or you can choose acceptance. You don't have to pretend that you're not angry. See the anger. Welcome it. Sit with it, feel it, acknowledge it, express it, and only then will it shift. Take your time to do it now."

"Okay."

"Can you see your anger?"

"Yes."

"What does it look like?"

"It's hideous. It's like a fiery beast. It looks like a dragon."

"Welcome in your anger and sit with it. Stay with it. Don't hide from it, don't try and run from it. Stare at it in the eyes; let it breathe all over you; let it burn you with its seething rage. Feel it … release it throughout your body. Become completely aware of it and let out a blood-curdling scream. All your anger needs to be expressed. It cannot stay inside you; you must free it. Yell, scream, punch. Do whatever you need to but do not suppress it!"

"Okay, but I'm furious."

"That's okay."

"All right, here goes."

I did as she said. I went deep into the edge of my rage. Everything went black and I let out a blood-curdling scream. I was so angry. I could feel rage rising from the depths of my soul. I began moving my body and shaking the energy out of me. Like a werewolf on a full moon I howled. I fell to my knees and began banging my fists on the earth. I was yelling and crying for a long time until it began to ease. I curled up in a foetal position and let sorrow pour out of my broken heart. After some time, I began to sigh and comfort myself. I began to feel better and I smiled as I stared at the sky.

"Have you heard of the Ho'oponopono?"

"The what?" I looked up at my higher self, the woman I was destined to be.

"No, I haven't"

"It's a four-step process created by a Hawaiian therapist called Dr Len."

"I have no idea what you're talking about."

"It's perfect for releasing all your anger to do with Sam. The first step is to say, 'I'm sorry'."

"For what?"

"You need to take responsibility for creating the situation. Your consciousness, which is made up of your thoughts, feelings and belief system brought this experience into being. Try it and see what happens."

"I'm sorry for hating you Sam and for blaming you for everything. I'm sorry for judging and despising you. I'm responsible for what happened, just as much as you are, and I'm sorry for wishing you ill."

"Now ask for forgiveness. Say, 'Please forgive me'."

"Please forgive me Sam for being so angry and hating you so much; for not taking responsibility for this and for focusing on all the negative things that have happened. Forgive me for being so angry and bitter. Forgive me for making you wrong and for not accepting you as you are. Forgive me for not seeing that you are doing the best you can."

"Now say, 'Thank you'. It doesn't matter who or what you are thanking."

"Thank you, Sam, for the time we've shared and for the love I experienced. Thank you for being a part of my journey, the good and the bad. Thank you to my heart for being able to let go and accept all that has come to pass. Thank you to my body for releasing all the emotion stuck inside me."

"Next you say, 'I love you'. You could be saying it to the person or to yourself."

"I love you Sam. I love you Ruby. I forgive you. I love the world. I love you all."

Silent tears of release began to stream from my eyes as I experienced the power of the Ho'oponopono.

"Take as long as you need. Let it all go now."

"Thank you. I feel so much better now."

"Life will shift in whatever direction you move it. If you think it is a rollercoaster, it will be one. If you think it is easy, it will be. So, the question starts with you. How do you want your life to be?"

"I want to create a powerful, happy life with a man that loves me."

"Then start believing it is possible. Think that it is, say that it is, feel that it is and, before you realise what is happening, it just is. If you continue to claim otherwise and react to life instead of allowing life to flow through you, then yes, your life will be a roller coaster – a roller coaster of reactions because, whatever you react to, flares up again and again until it is healed."

"Yes, that is so true. If I resist letting go and forgiving what has happened, the experience will continue to persist."

"In this program you will become more than the stream of thoughts bombarding you day-in and day-out. You will build yourself into a powerful creator of divine experiences.

"Now I'm going to give you a quick lesson on self-love and treating yourself with respect."

"Self-love is something that I really struggle with."

"Yes, I know. Are you ready?"

"Yes."

Chapter 4

SELF-LOVE

Ruby Rose, I want you to imagine a symbol in your mind or a picture that represents your feelings about yourself.

"Okay."

"What do you see?"

"A dirty pool of water, slime and sludge. It stinks and smells like something has died."

"In a moment I'm going to ask you to completely transform this and create a symbol that represents absolute freedom. Are you ready to do that?

"Yes!"

"Great! I want you to imagine a symbol; it might be a cross, a star or a golden sun – something that represents you being free. Can you see something?"

"My symbol of freedom is a dove."

"Imagine your body is being transformed into a sacred temple and place the symbol of the dove above your head. Shine your truth into the world."

"I am a temple of peace and my body is devoted to self-love."

"Would you let someone with dirty shoes enter your temple?"

"No."

"If you like things clean and organised, are you going to let someone come in and make a mess of your temple?"

"No!"

"Then hold your temple strong by putting up boundaries around yourself. Say this now:

I cast out anything in my temple that no longer serves me.

Anything not of the light be gone now from this time and space.
All negative thoughts and feelings that I'm carrying are banished.
"Invite purity into your temple. Say:
White light, blue ray, violet flame, protection.
"Say it three times."
White light, blue ray, violet flame, protection.
White light, blue ray, violet flame, protection.
White light, blue ray, violet flame, protection.

"Close your eyes and see your temple; see your symbol as a beacon above your head. What colours do you see?"

"My dove is white, and the holy spirit of love is emanating from all around."

"What colour is your temple?"

"My temple is pastel blue."

"Say this now,
I am a temple of peace.
Repeat it three times and see the symbol above your head; notice how your body responds to your words."

I am a temple of peace.
I am a temple of peace.
I am a temple of peace.

"The dove is centred at the top of my temple with a golden light around it and when I say, I am a temple of peace, the bird begins to fly and the golden light showers all around me. Beautiful light is pouring into the top of my head and my whole body is filling with peace. I feel like a queen standing tall. I feel beautiful, special and peaceful now."

"Expand your sentence from I am a temple of peace and add some words to create who you are."

"I am a temple of peace, love and truth. I surrender to the light."

"Why did you choose those things?"

"I want to feel peace in accepting life exactly as it is. Love in giving and receiving, truth in being authentic to my word and surrender in feeling safe to let go of my mind. I want to flow with life and let life be whatever it is meant to be. I don't want to hold on anymore, I want to live in peace. LIP! Live in Peace!"

"See how your truth is becoming clear. We call it your 'essence'."

"My essence?"

"Yes, the real you. You are a queen of peace."

"I feel so content when I see myself this way."

"This is the power of focus and connecting to your truth. You choose your state when you focus on what makes you feel good. Your natural state is to be peaceful. Your fearful state chooses you when your thoughts lack focus. Always make your intentions clear."

"What do you mean by intentions?"

"Your intention is your focused outcome. Yours is peace. You said it clearly at the start. "I am a temple of peace." We use "I am" because it is powerfully anchored in the here and now. I would never advise you to say, I want to be a temple of peace. You will never reach that state until you claim it. I am, makes it so. The same with "I choose". Choosing something gives you freedom. Try saying 'I choose the abortion'.

I hesitated, immediately feeling resistance. Anger at Sam was resurfacing. "He made me do it. If it weren't for him, I would have had the baby."

"You aren't taking responsibility for your actions and now you are disempowering yourself by blaming him for the choice that you made."

I was furious that she was holding me accountable.

"Just try saying it."

"What?"

"I choose the abortion."

"I choose the abortion."

"What do you notice?"

"There's a sense of relief in my body as though I can finally relax. You are right. I do feel more empowered because I am taking responsibility for my choice."

"Choosing the pain in your life creates acceptance. When you state your intention: 'I am a temple of peace' you give your word to it and there is power in your word. Then you feel it in your body, and you become it. Using this technique gives you the opportunity to create positive thoughts and feelings in any moment that you choose. Is there anything more that you would like to intentionally create for yourself?"

"Yes, a bright and exciting future."

"Okay, wonderful. So, use the power of your word to create a statement that you can tap into on an emotional level and really feel the feelings as you say what you want."

I looked at her and felt shy, but my heart was excited by the idea that I could create powerful feelings by simply choosing them. I took a deep breath and gave it a go. I cleared my throat and nervously started.

"I am the master of my temple and only thoughts of the highest order connected to my health and wellbeing reside here."

She beamed at me and I instantly felt inspired. I was gaining momentum and confidence.

"I am the queen of my kingdom; love and light abide here. I reign in peace, prosperity and love!"

"Great! Notice how you're getting creative with it. That's perfect. Yes! Why not make yourself the queen of your inner kingdom! That's your choice and you are a creator! Well done. Close your eyes and be in your kingdom. Let's create your bright and exciting future. Imagine that you have found the highest vantage point in your kingdom."

"Okay, I am climbing to the top of the castle tower and looking out beyond the castle walls."

"What can you see in the distance?"

"I'm reaching the highest mountain, and all my hopes and dreams are coming true."

"As the sun casts its golden hues across the lands, what promise will you make to yourself today?"

"I promise to be the queen of my kingdom and to focus my undivided attention on thoughts that make me feel good. I want to make all my dreams come true and fulfil my reason for being here. I want to make peace with who I am."

"Beautiful, I love it."

"So, do I! It's so exciting!"

"May I say a prayer for you to complete your manifestation?"

"Manifestation? What's that?"

"When we ask for what we want and then it comes to us in physical form, we call that a manifestation."

"Okay, great. Yes please, I would love that."

In the name of love, I pray for you. May you connect to your inner source of unconditional love and begin to feel deep peace within you, as you see the truth of who you are.

I pray that you understand that there is no separation and there is no loss. I pray that you are one with your true self. May you begin to hold this knowledge within you and know yourself as perfect, whole and complete. May you become connected to all that you are.

May you attune your senses and awareness to the infinite pulse that beats within all things. May you speak the language of love and always be forgiving in your words and actions. May you know that the universe is always supporting you and that the energy that creates worlds is flowing through you.

In the name of love, I pray that you feel deep peace within you and that you are free of the things that separate you from who you are. I pray in the name of love that you never sacrifice who you are or your dreams. I pray that you surrender to self-love in all things.

I pray that pure love fills your heart with faith and trust. I pray that you intuitively understand that all things are coming to you in perfect timing and in divine order. I pray that you see that your lessons are your blessings and that you can trust this implicitly when challenges present themselves to you.

May you stay connected to your faith and practise the power of prayer. May you use the power of the word in this way to raise the broken hearts of the planet. May you be the light that shines for others who are in darkness. I ask that you fear nothing and that you surrender now to your inner being; your spirit of love. I ask that you connect to your inner light and let it fill you. May you sing with praise and joy in your heart. May your offerings be kind and sweet.

"Repeat after me;

I am loved, I am loved, I am loved. I repeated the words.

"To receive is to be in grace with love and you are loved."

"Thank you," I said, looking at her magnificence with gratitude.

"For what?"

"For coming back for me, I've been so lost and afraid."

"I've never left you. I am always with you. I am your higher self."

I could feel love pouring into me and strengthening me. She was inspiring me with courage, determination, power and purpose. I began to feel taller, broader and more expansive. As I looked up, I began to grow towards the light like a tree.

The blue sky was enveloping me and I felt limitless, like the butterfly. I had my own pair of emerald wings and I was moving effortlessly through the air. I felt the presence of my true self within me, and I began to glide higher and higher. The spirit of love was bedazzling me with a childlike sense of magic and wonder. I began to sing:

"I am loved. I am loved. I am loved! Oh, my goodness, it is true, I am loved!"

"You're doing it, well done! You're trusting in your faith to take you above all that is an illusion. You are raising your vibration. You are making progress. Do you feel ready to see the memory from your childhood that is creating the root cause of your suffering?"

"I think so."

"You are ready! Let's get started. Lie down here on the grass as I take you back into your earliest memory."

Chapter 5

FLASHBACK

I was sitting on the back steps of my rustic house, looking up at the Australian gum trees standing tall, like giants above me. I was watching them sway gently back and forth in the summer breeze. I lowered my gaze from the tree-lined sky to the pages tucked in my lap and absorbed the colourful images in the book I was reading.

My eyes widened with excitement, as I turned the page to see two lovers taking their first kiss. A handsome prince was dancing with a beautiful princess and their eyes were locked together in a loving gaze. The woman's blue eyes matched her elegant ball gown and she looked stunning with her blonde hair and slim figure. The prince was tall, dark and handsome. He had mesmerising hazel eyes.

I held my hands to my heart with delight, as I eagerly turned another page but the sound of my parents fighting distracted me from the fairy-tale I was reading.

"Why are you drinking coffee?" I heard my mother say.

"Because I want to," my father grumbled.

I rubbed my eyes and felt the beginnings of a frown creasing my forehead. Feelings of unease started in the pit of my stomach. I began to shuffle my body – braced for another fight.

"You know coffee is bad for you," my mother insisted.

"I don't care," my father said, becoming agitated at being told what to do.

"It's a drug," she persisted, unwilling to let the issue go.

"I know!" The irritation in his voice increased.

"Then why do you drink it?" she demanded.

Spiritual Spring

"Because I want to! Why don't you stop telling me what to do and leave me be?"

"Well you should stop drinking coffee!" she insisted.

"Go away, will ya! I've had enough! Just leave me alone. I'll make up my own mind, thanks. Let me drink my coffee in peace!"

"I will not! Not when you speak to me like that."

"Well, you don't hear a word I say!" My father sounded frustrated.

"See what coffee does to you. It makes you angry. It's poisoning you."

"I don't care! Will you give it up already?"

"No, I won't! It's not good for you and you need to stop drinking it."

"Well, what about you? You drink too much tea."

"What's wrong with tea? It's full of antioxidants."

"You shouldn't have so many cups."

"Who says?"

"I do."

"Well, I'm not going to listen to you."

"Then why do you expect me to listen to you!"

"You never listen to anything I tell you anyway."

"Oh, here we go again."

"Yes, but when are you going to stop drinking alcohol?"

"I'm not going to stop until you leave me alone."

My dad was really starting to fire up as my mother expressed her concerns. I put my hands around my ears and stared at the fairy-tale picture book. I didn't want to hear my mother and father's angry squabbling anymore. I turned the pages in the book with my little hands and, instead of listening to my parents fighting, I looked at the bright, happy pictures in the love story. I couldn't read the words yet, but the pictures told me very clearly that the prince and the princess were deeply in love and that my mother and father were not.

I love my mother and father. Why don't they love each other? Why aren't they happy? Why don't they look like the people in the book? A single salty tear fell from my eyes, landing between the beautiful lady with the golden hair and the handsome man. Their gaze was so magical and their smiles so bright. Sparkles of light moved between them as they stared into each other's eyes. They were dancing in a beautiful ballroom with people all around them and they looked so happy.

I want the story with the prince and the princess! Not my mum and dad fighting every morning! Hearing the door slam from the kitchen, my body relaxed. The fight was over. My father stormed outside to drink his coffee in peace. He was probably heading to the garden to tend to his lettuces.

I crossed my pinkie fingers together and made a promise to myself. I'm never going to be like my mother and father. I'm never going to live like them. I'm going to have a fairy-tale life, and I'm going to live happily ever after with my very own handsome prince.

I closed the page on a sparkly slipper, abandoned on a staircase with a pumpkin carriage fleeing the scene. I put the book away. I needed to get away. The heaviness had spread from my stomach, into my heart. I knew the only thing that would make me feel better was to run down the road.

I got up off the steps and glanced one last time at the book I'd been reading. I sighed to myself sadly and walked around to the front of the house. I could feel the smooth mossy texture of the grass beneath my feet, hardening as it turned to gravel. The rhythm of my steps and the flow of movement in my tiny body helped me breathe more easily. I looked at the surrounding Australian bushland of gum trees, tea tree and dogwood. No-one but my four sisters and I ever heard our parents fighting. The closest neighbour lived a kilometre away. I began to jog down the road, trying to escape the memory of my parents, but my mind was still disturbed by troubling feelings.

A lightbulb went off in my head as I thought of the different ways, I could stop them fighting. If I could fix my parents' problems and make everyone happy, maybe things would get better for all of us. Maybe I was the problem! That must be it! It was my fault that they were fighting, and I was to blame! It was all my fault. I did something wrong, which was making them unhappy. I was responsible.

As the gravel twisted around the bend, I ran past the chook house. I could hear the clucking of the hens, pecking the grass as they searched for worms. It reminded me to check for eggs on my way back home. As I picked up speed, the blossoming tea tree looked like a blur of white snowflakes. As I rounded the corner, the foliage changed drastically, into a haven of lush green man ferns. My sisters and I called this place Moss Land and it was a magical spot to play and build cubbies. The entire area was covered in moss, and we were always collecting treasures and special things. It was our favourite spot, on our sixty-four acres of land because it was so special.

As I zoomed past Moss Land and raced up the hill, I passed "dead man's track". I glanced to the left and down the perilous bike path. It was very slippery. We called it "dead man's track" because, late one school night when Dad was blind drunk, we heard him screaming through the bush, as he flew down the muddy slopes. He'd bounced over the bumps and jumps and skidded through all the watery slips but still managed to stay in one piece.

All of us girls had held our breath that night, hoping he wouldn't have an accident like the time he fell into an open bonfire at a party and burnt his entire body. He seemed to have a habit of engaging in dangerous behaviour while he was drunk. He'd drink himself into a stupor and then drive us home from the party. Emma, my older sister, always sat with him in the front seat, making sure he stayed on the road. Thanks to her looking out for us, he always managed to get us kids home safe. But without us in the car, he often crashed.

My pace increased as the road levelled out and my stride began to lengthen. I usually ran to the neighbour's house and back. As soon as I heard the neighbour's dogs barking, I always turned around and ran home. I didn't want Tom thinking I was a stranger, trespassing on his property. I'd seen him with his shotgun before, making sure people weren't lurking around on his land.

Chapter 5: Flashback

My heart began to race as I heard a gun being fired. Not by my neighbour this time, but in my memory. Time and space flashed before me. My steps on the gravel dissolved into steps on my school oval as memories from my recent school cross-country came flooding back to me. I heard the voice of the principal calling all five-year-old girls to the starting line.

"Okay, girls the race is about to start. On your marks, get set, go!" The sound of the gun shot took me by surprise, but I was off and racing in my cross-country event. It was a long-distance race and I was wearing a yellow T-shirt for Imbru, my school team. People were cheering me on: "Go Ruby Rose!"

The 2 km track took us all over the primary school, around the oval, past the local shop which sold the yummy hot chips I loved so much, and down a gravel road with big stones on the sides. My body moved with rhythm and the race came easy to me.

When I passed the finishing line, they handed me the first-place certificate. I stared at it in awe. My eyes widened with surprise. I won the race! I was the fastest five-year-old girl at Boat Harbour Primary School! I smiled to myself as the memory disappeared and I turned around on the gravel road. My feelings of heaviness were gone, and I felt happy again. My mind was clear. I began running back to the house.

Chapter 6

BIRTH

I'm bringing you back now from the memory of your childhood. Open your eyes and stretch." I opened my eyes as the memory disappeared. Loving eyes were staring at me.

"In a moment you are going to leave this beautiful garden. You are going to get back into the vessel and you will have two choices: to thrive in life or to barely survive. If you are prepared to discover who you really are, I suggest you press the button: ESA. This will continue your journey with the Ego and Spirit Adventure.

"If you are not ready, press C. Consciousness will take you back to the hospital. Remember, everything that you choose in this reality is as every bit as real as your normal reality. So, what do you want to do?"

"I'm not sure? A part of me feels afraid of the Ego and Spirit Adventure because you said it's only new and it is an experiment. What if something goes wrong?"

"You can make your decision by having a conversation with the Universal Mind if you like. All you have to do is ask, like this: "Dear Universal Mind, please allow me to explore this idea of who I truly am in a space that is free from fear – free from criticism and free from anything other than love.

I looked at her in shock.

"You've got to be kidding? You want me to speak to the Universal mind? C'mon, that is ridiculous. I've never even heard of such a thing."

"Why? What's so silly about it? Just try it."

"No way. I'm not trying it."

"Then, there is nothing more I can do for you. I was under the impression that you were wanting to find out who you are."

I was directed back into the vessel.

"You will wake up in your hospital bed and your procedure will have been successful. You will go back to being the way you've always been. You will repeat the same patterns and you will find another man who isn't going to love you the way you deserve. You will repeat the same cycle again and again until you finally learn. Our time is up. Please press the button now and it will take you back to level C."

"No! No! No! Please, I need your help! I can't do this alone. I need to find out who I am. If I go back now, I will mess everything up."

"Then ask your ego to relax. Ask for some space so you can do your inner work. Thank it for being so good to you and see what happens. That is all I am asking you to do."

"Seriously, this is the weirdest thing I've ever heard of, but I'll do it." I looked around sheepishly, feeling foolish and embarrassed but I was determined to find an answer to who I really was.

"Prepare yourself in the vessel, have a chat to the Universal Mind, and trust. That is all you need right now." She waved goodbye and left. I suddenly felt abandoned and alone.

The ESA button lit up and I stepped inside before the doors closed. The vessel started moving. I cleared my throat and asked the question I was secretly desperate to find out.

"Universal mind, who am I?"

A wise voice replied. "Who do you think you are?" I felt surprised by the voice but then again this was a very strange place.

"I'm not sure who I am Universal mind."

"If you vanish into thin air tomorrow and find yourself face to face with the energy of creation, who will you introduce yourself as?"

"I'll introduce myself as Ruby Rose."

"Is it possible that you're so preoccupied that you don't even know who you are?"

"Preoccupied?"

"Yes. What if all your possessions and achievements were to suddenly disappear, what's left?"

"Not much."

"Who exactly are you without your stuff?"

"I don't know."

"Who are you beyond your career, your education, your family and your life history?"

"I'm not sure."

"Who are you without the distractions or coping mechanisms that you use to survive life?"

"I don't know? Material things make me feel important. The expensive car, the house, a marriage with kids, a career and security are all that matters. It's what I've been aiming for my whole life."

"Why are you aiming for it?"

"Because then I'll be important."

"Who says you're not important now?"

"I do."

"Why does having "things" suddenly make you someone?"

"Because I'll fit in and I'll be like everybody else."

"Is that what you want? To fit in?"

"Yes, I want to be loved and I want to be accepted."

"Do you realise that even if you have those things, you won't necessarily feel loved and there is no guarantee that you will be accepted."

"Why?"

"Because they're ideas you've invented about life. They're made-up stories you're telling yourself that you believe to be true. At some point in your life, you decided that having "things" was the answer to happiness. You started looking around at what everybody else was doing and you noticed that they were preoccupied by the same "things" too – owning a house, getting married, having children. Has it ever occurred to you, that you've become completely distracted by the world around you?"

"Not until now."

"Then, don't look to the outside world to find an answer of who you are. The Creator will ask you to look within yourself. Searching outside of yourself is an attempt to fill the emptiness inside you, which is masking a void."

"A void?"

"Yes, it's the feeling that you're missing out on something or that if you could find someone to love you, then you would be complete, but it's not true."

"Why not? If someone loves me, then I will feel complete."

"You're feeding an illusion. What you really need to find out are answers to these questions: What gives you a sense of purpose? What fills you with inspiration? What do you stand for and how are you going to make a difference in the world? The world needs you to step up. It's time for leadership. Are you willing to be vulnerable, raw and honest?"

"I'm not sure."

"Just to let you know, as you begin questioning yourself in this way, it will challenge your "identity" and your sense of "I", otherwise known as your ego, will feel threatened. Your ego will feel like it's losing control because it doesn't believe that it's safe for you to be vulnerable. Your false sense of self has been running the show for so long that you believe you need to wear a mask to protect your true feelings. It's been so busy looking out for your survival, that it will sabotage your success."

"Why?"

"Because at the crux of your ego's existence is fear. This consciousness has cleverly made its way into your mind. It feeds you with panic and anxiety to the point that it takes control of your wellbeing and makes you feel sick.

Deep-rooted issues are controlling your happiness. You are not operating as your authentic self because fear is driving your decisions. The world around you isn't helping either. Magazines, TV shows and the media appeal to the wounded aspects of your human condition.

Many of you are suffering because you don't feel loved or good enough. You don't feel safe that life has your back and that things will work out for you. You lack the courage to trust and surrender into the unknown and push past your limitations."

"That's so true! Beauty magazines make me feel ugly and make me think I need to get breast implants."

"That's because your ego has an inflation problem, it likes to be liked, it likes to look good and it wants to be admired. You are not alone. There is a need inside every human being to feel important and to be recognised, but there is also a greater purpose to your existence and that is to evolve and grow. This is when life becomes meaningful.

"If you contribute to the world in a way that feels positive and makes a difference, then you will find fulfilment. However small or large that looks, it doesn't matter. Just being you is enough. Even if all you focus on is being your authentic self, that will be enough."

"What if I don't know what my authentic self looks like?"

"That's ok, this program will show you. You shy away from drawing too much attention to yourself because you lack the belief that you are worthy of love. This negative self-image hinders your personal growth and stops you from living your truth.

"When you ignore your inner being and stop trusting your internal guidance system, you actually miss out on the magic that is waiting for you – the magic that you already know exists.

"Within you is a wounded part that is holding you hostage right now. It's your inner child and, until you remember to hear her, hold her and comfort her, you will never reach the truth of who you really are because you will stay stuck in your pain – your childish insecurity and her holding patterns. You need to face your deepest wounds. The ones from your childhood, from your parents and your lineage. You must look into your ancestry to release old patterns."

"Will I be able to do that in this program?"

"Many answers lie here but that is all we have time for because it's time for you to begin your Ego and Spirit Adventure. You need to ask your mind for some time and space to begin this process. Good luck, I hope you experience an awakening. I believe in you."

"Thank you, Universal Mind."

"You are welcome." I felt the silence instantly and I knew I was on my own.

"Mind? Can you hear me? Are you listening? Are you there? I know this sounds weird, but I am grateful for all the thinking that you've been doing for me. I don't think I've ever stopped to acknowledge and appreciate you. You are literally thinking something every second of the day. It's incredible all the analysing, organising, interpreting, arranging, decoding and deciphering that you do. I feel silly talking to you like this, but I want to give you a holiday. I'm giving you a chance to sit back and relax. Not for too long! Because you are very important to me, but long enough for you to slow down, rest and relax. How does that sound? I'm safe and there is no danger."

"It sounds good to me, thank you."

My mind responded as the vessel I was travelling in slowed and came to a gentle stop. The doors opened and I released a suspended breath and exhaled with relief as my mind flooded with gratitude. I had no idea my mind was so responsive to suggestions. My mind sent me a flush of happiness and obediently left.

I stepped out of the vessel into the Ego and Spirit Adventure. I could see a wide-open space with volcanoes stretching across a barren landscape. It looked like a beautiful desert dotted with fire-breathing mountains. I took a deep breath in and I let go. A sense of peace and stillness expanded my awareness. Every inhalation of air and every exhalation felt soft, gentle and light.

Suddenly, the volcanoes stopped erupting and bright red lava began sliding down their rocky faces. A flush of heat spread over my face as beads of perspiration began running in tiny streams down my forehead.

I blinked in awe as a magical butterfly began dancing toward me. I recognised my own nature within it. Its grace and lightness mirrored my own.

Chapter 6: Birth

"The light within you, is the same light within me.

"We are always connected, because we are one and the same."

Wonder overwhelmed me as I began to align with my spirit awakening inside me. I felt myself lifting above the colourful hues of the landscape. I began dissolving into a formless state of freedom. I was feeling free from the density of my physical form. Free from my past and free from my pain. Everything was dropping away.

As I flew higher and higher, I felt my heart opening.

I know who I am.

I am a being of love and light.

I am the essence of the divine.

I am a source for good.

I am one with all that is and all that ever will be.

I am, I am, I am.

Yes, I know who I am.

I am love; I am light.

I am a butterfly; I am the sky.

I am limitless and I am free.

I know who I am.

Who I am is good.

I am a force for love and all good things come to me.

I am a magnet for peace.

I am a magnet for light.

I breathe deep and I am at ease.

I am ready open and willing to trust.

To receive abundance, positivity and hope.

I am willing to allow inspiration to align with my higher purpose.

I am open and willing to dream again.

I am open to receive love now.

I am a force for good.

"Hey! I'm back!" The voice of Ego shook me from the spirit of love opening within me.

"Oh no! I was just experiencing something divine, Ego."

"Well ... I took a little rest and then I thought you might need me. You know that question, who are you? I have the answer you're looking for. Your name is Ruby Rose Taylor, you are a female, you have four sisters and a mother and a father. You were born on the family property in Lapoinya, Tasmania, at 3am on November 1 in 1981. You were taught to read and write at Boat Harbour Primary School. Then you went to Wynyard High School. After completing college, you gained a Bachelor of Fine Arts at university. You majored in photography and then became a qualified primary school teacher."

"Oh, Ego! Stop it! Why did you come back so soon? I was just getting a sense of who I am, without all those types of distractions. I'm not looking for the answer in an analytical, categorised or structured way!"

Ego looked annoyed and began to argue back.

"Don't waste your time on that fluffy stuff. These are the facts. This is the truth of who you are. Besides ... I didn't have anything to do ... I thought you might need me and, if I wasn't around to protect you, you might go and hurt yourself again."

"No, Ego. Don't do that thing you do ..."

"What?" Ego looked flabbergasted and confused.

"Don't assume that you know what I'm thinking or feeling. Just ask me next time. I'm enjoying the inspiration program with the spirit of love. I'm feeling something I've never felt before. It's like I've experienced a glimpse of my truth. I'm seeing things with new eyes and I can finally breathe. I feel trapped and constrained by your definition of who I am. I'm starting to experience a sense of something beyond my mind and it feels marvellous. It feels incredible. But I lost it the moment you came back."

"What are you saying? You don't need me anymore?" Ego sounded devastated.

"No ... of course not ... but can you see the difference? If you relax more, Ego, I can experience true freedom."

"Mm, I don't know ..."

"Look, Ego, I've never been educated to connect with who I really am. All my life, I've been taught identity-based principles by society — a society that operates and is dominated by mental consciousness. I've been educated by a system of thinking that focuses on doing rather than simply being. I've become so focused on being right all the time that I've been making others wrong."

"Yes, and what is wrong with being right all the time?" Ego looked confused.

"Because it's a power play, Ego, and I'm really in a battle with myself. I've tried to fabricate an identity by buying things because I thought I'd be accepted but my life is a façade, based on my deep feelings of unworthiness."

"Yeah, but that's good because you will be loved if you have those things and people will want to be around you."

I paused and really thought about what Ego was saying.

"I might be loved?" I looked at Ego with open eyes.

"Yes, you might be loved."

"Ego, you are already loved! Beyond all the possessions in this world. Beyond this physical realm, you are everything you already need to be. Right before you came back, I felt it. I was feeling whole."

"No! You're lying because the truth is, I'm unlovable." Ego's walls were cracking apart and ripples of emotion were beginning to swell within.

My enlivened spirit continued, "No, Ego that's not true, you are lovable. You are perfect and you are whole. You are all knowing, and you are complete. You are the butterfly – limitless and free."

"Oh, stop it! I know you are only trying to help, but I don't believe you. I need approval and love from others all the time and, to get it, I try to please people. I'm so afraid that I'm nobody. I try and pretend like I'm someone, but deep down the truth is, I'm nothing and I don't belong anywhere.

"I'm empty and hollow. I put walls up around me and I never let anyone too close because I'm afraid if they get to know the real me then they'll discover that I'm a fraud, I'm a fake and that there is nothing to see. There is nothing to love and then they will know my secret; they will know that I am unlovable."

"So, you don't feel loved? Is that the problem?"

"Yes! I don't love myself and I'm afraid I won't be liked for who I am. I'm afraid I'll never amount to anything, so I try to please everyone all the time, but then I get angry and annoyed. I feel used. I act all nice to people's faces, but I don't have the courage to tell them how I really feel and so I keep making the same mistakes. I keep following the same patterns. I want everything to be perfect. I judge myself first and then I judge others." I looked at Ego and gently took Ego's hand.

"Would you like me to help you, Ego? Would you like me to show you how deeply loved you are so that you never forget? Would you like me to contact someone whom I know will help you?"

Ego looked at me with hesitation and disbelief.

"You would do that for me?"

"Yes, I love you, Ego, I'll do anything I can to help you and I will dedicate my life to you, if it means helping you to see that together we can be whole. Would you like that, Ego? Would you like to feel the freedom of being loved?"

Ego burst into tears. All the pretending, the pain and the fear was finally revealed.

"All I've ever wanted is to feel whole. Most of the time I feel separate, isolated, lonely and unloved. You know my whole life; I've been trying to find a way to feel good. I've used alcohol, drugs, sex, gambling, possessions and obsessions. You name it, I've tried it. The whole time, I've been searching for a way to feel good about myself, but it's hard, because it never lasts. I would really love your help; I am so tired of feeling like this."

Okay, Ego, I'm more than happy to help you. How would you like to be given the secret pin code to feeling completely loved?

"A secret pin code? Yeah, sure that sounds fun!"

"Great! You mentioned before that you are struggling with your self-esteem. I want you to know that you deserve to feel loved, because you are lovable, and you are good enough. Completing this part of the program involves teaching you to connect to a higher state of consciousness. Are you willing to do that?"

"I'm not sure what that means but yes, I am willing to try it!"

Chapter 6: Birth

"Great, let's do it now."

Chapter 7

FREEDOM

"I'm going to show you how to access freedom from fear. You can use it anywhere you like, because it's free."

"If it's completely free and I can access it anywhere I like, can I do it now?"

"Yes, you can!"

"Well, what are we waiting for. I want to try it!"

"Perfect!" I exclaimed, amazed at the change in Ego. Ego's face was beginning to soften as a hopeful ray of light began to spread through the darkness. It was like watching a rainbow form after an ominous downpour.

"Okay, I need some details from you. Can you give me the first four digits of your birth date?"

"I was born on November 1, 1981, so that means 1111."

"All you have to do is say your numbers out loud. There are many universal providers that you can connect with, so you need to choose one that feels right for you. Then, we can make an agreement with that one."

Ego eyed me suspiciously,

"An agreement? You're not going to sting me at the end of this, are you? Please don't tell me there are hidden costs or sign-up fees. I don't like surprises! It's happened to me before and I can tell you that if it happens again, I will not be impressed. Those marketing companies are rip-off merchants and you can't trust them. Everyone is out for themselves. They're all liars! I like to know what I'm getting myself into before I sign a contract."

I interrupted Ego from ranting any further,

"Umm, Ego, like I said, it's completely free. There are no sign-up fees or hidden costs. You're complicating it now by attaching your past to it. Can you move from this space of fear and get present again? I lost you for a second."

"Oh ... sorry! Woah, I don't know what came over me? So, how much did you say this contract was going to cost?"

"Ego! It's free. I'm not trying to sell you anything, and it's not a contract! You have free will to use it as much or as little as you like."

"Well then, is it even going to work?"

"Oh wow, Ego. Can you stop for a second? I'm finding it very difficult to communicate with you. You're going at a hundred miles per second. Can you please calm down?"

"Calm down? How am I supposed to calm down when I'm not in control! I don't know what's going on. I don't even know what's happening. You were the one saying that I was entering into an agreement."

"Yes, let me clarify. By opening to this type of connection you are agreeing to connect to the source of all that is. Are you in agreement with that? By doing this, you will be able to receive information to help remove the programs that contain your limiting beliefs?"

"Oh, okay, that sounds fine! Sorry, I jumped the gun and started imagining the worst."

"It's okay. You're out of your comfort zone. Did you notice how quickly your fears and doubts came up? Do you remember what it felt like right before the fear and uncertainty took over? What were you feeling grateful for?"

"Um ...where was I? Oh yeah! I was feeling grateful that you were willing to help me."

Ego looked at me rather sheepishly.

"I was feeling happy because you said you were going to help me believe that I am good enough and that I am loved."

"Yes! That's right and do you still want those things?"

Chapter 7: Freedom

"I don't know, Spirit. It all seems too hard; I think I've changed my mind. I really appreciate your offer, but I don't think I'm ready yet."

"So, you're not ready yet?"

No, I don't think so."

"Okay, so what seems to be the problem?"

"Oh, well you know…"

"No, I don't know …"

"I really want to but …"

"Yes? You really want to … but?"

"Well, umm … the truth is…" Ego whispered with wounded vulnerability.

"The truth is?"

"Oh, this is stupid …"

"No, it's not, c'mon you're almost there."

"The truth is, I'm afraid."

"You're afraid?"

"Yes, I am afraid."

"Ego, can I ask you something?"

"Yes, of course."

"Is there a time in your life when you haven't been afraid?"

Ego looked at me, painfully aware there wasn't.

"No, not really."

"Do you think you're ready to choose your universal provider now?"

"How do I know which one to trust?"

"If you stay bogged down by the fear of the unknown, then you will miss the gifts that are waiting for you on the other side of fear. You need to be willing to step past your fears and your resistance by learning to trust in life."

"I find it really challenging, Spirit, I don't want to keep making the same mistakes."

"It's okay to feel what you feel, but check to see if the danger is real. Is there a fire burning in your house? Are your thoughts taking you away from feeling positive and open to new experiences? That's all you have to do; just ask yourself a quick question like: Why does it fill me with so much anxiety? Am I going to die? Is it threatening my survival?

"Try saying this now:

I release all my habitual thought patterns of fear and anxiety that do not serve me in this moment. I command these feelings to be gone now from my mind. Anything not of the light be gone now from this time and space. All love and light now to me, all love and light now to me.

"Okay, it sounds really empowering, I'll try it!

I release all my habitual thought patterns of fear and anxiety that do not serve me in this moment. I command these feelings to be gone now from my mind. Anything not of the light be gone now from this time and space.

All love and light now to me, all love and light now to me.

Ego took in a deep breath.

"You've just learnt one of the steps to clear your energy before you make the call to your universal provider. All you need to do now is type in your pin code, which I explained earlier."

"Oh, what was it again? I forgot!"

"Ego? Are you serious ...?"

"I'm sorry ... my mind was wandering down the road with fear and I can't remember what you said. You wouldn't believe how hard it is to focus when I feel anxious. Do you know what it's like, Spirit, to lose concentration?"

I stared at Ego blankly.

"No, I'm sorry, Ego, I have no idea what you're talking about, and I've never experienced such a thing!"

"Are you serious?" Ego looked at me with a glare of envy and started to turn green with anger and outrage.

I felt an uncontrollable urge to laugh, which didn't make Ego very happy.

"What! You mean to say, you've never lost focus in your life?"

"No, I don't operate in the mind."

"You've never been scrolling through Facebook or Instagram and a couple of hours later wonder why you are on the internet in the first place? You mean to tell me that you don't understand the concept of losing focus? Tell me, Spirit, what else don't you understand the concept of? I'm intrigued."

"Well, Ego, I don't understand why this is taking so long. I exist beyond time and space, I just am. I feel drained by all this procrastination because it seems like an awful waste of ... what word would you use? Time!"

"Don't you have time, Spirit?"

"Time doesn't exist in all dimensions. I am eternal and therefore I don't work on time frames. Linear time is a constructed reality created in the fourth dimension.

"What?"

"Ego, I'm going to try one last thing with you. If it doesn't work, I guess it means we've both failed this program, please help me because I really need to succeed at this before I go back to consciousness."

"Okay!"

"I was just wondering, what things put you in a really good mood?"

"What puts me in a good mood? I know, when I win. I really love to win! I love to feel like I'm the best! When the losers are underneath me, I feel like I'm on top of the world. I don't care if I have to kick them to the curb to beat them. If they're in my way, I'll stand on them, push them and throw them to the side. That's me, Spirit, I'm the winner." Ego puffed up and strode forward with the arrogance of a bull.

"Ego, would you say you're a spiritual being?"

"Spiritual? No way, not one bit! I don't believe in God ... well, hang on. What exactly do you mean when you say 'spiritual'? I don't want people to label me as narrow-minded, but I'm certainly not a Christian or Muslim, either. My father was dead against all that religious stuff."

"Whether people want to acknowledge it or not," I said, "we are all experiencing some form of spiritual existence and everyone has an opportunity to explore it. No matter how little it is spoken of, or collectively recognised, it is a force that all humans choose to acknowledge or remain confused by.

"A spiritual person is no better if they are condemning those who have not connected to their soul; neither is the non-spiritual person who judges those who are spiritual. There is no right or wrong, higher or lower. It is with unconditional love and acceptance that we open our hearts and expand our minds to all people.

"All human beings are worthy of love. Love is the common thread that wraps around us. We are surrounded by a greater mystery, an infinite web that connects us to the power of love."

"Well then, Spirit, now that you have my attention, what is it all about? What does it mean to be spiritual?"

"People who are spiritual are inspired. The word 'inspired' means to be in spirit. To be in spirit is a state of freedom, flow and trust. Have you ever felt inspired, Ego?"

Ego stared at me, dazed with a grumpy look.

"Umm ...," Ego shrugged and looked blankly at the ground, breathing a sigh of disappointment. "Umm, uhh, I really don't know what you mean?"

"I mean inspired ..."

"Inspired ... inspired ... inspired?" Ego kept repeating it and started walking around. I'd say it's like being captivated by a thought – a thought that basks in your mind like a light. It's like a beacon shining into your heart that has the power to spread. Oh, yes! It spreads so fast that you feel as though your entire being is taking off with an idea!

"Thoughts transcend time and space and I feel as though I can do anything! Absolutely anything is possible when those seeds of inspiration hit! They're like little diamonds of opportunity glinting in the sun. They're so special and profound, it's like a crystal sky is sparkling in my mind."

"Yes, Ego, that's it! Your mind is a sky of possibility and, as your ideas begin to take shape, they're like seeds of desire sprouting towards you, giving you what you truly want – awakening something inside you."

"Yes! It's like a well of water that suddenly breaks free. A great surge of energy and movement shifts, and I get an idea to do something. That's right! I do know moments like this and they're useless! They are complete and utter nonsense; they are for dreamers, Spirit! They are for people who have lost touch with reality. 'Dreamers' waste their time chasing fruitless ideas and never amount to anything. They have no money, no house and no car! They have nothing, Spirit, so what's the good of it? If you have nothing to show for it, what's the point?" I looked at Ego,

"Nothing to show for it, hey? Can you tell me something, Ego? How are you feeling right now?"

Ego's face had turned purple and his fists were knotted into tiny stumps, curled up tight like a newborn struggling to expel wind.

"I am really peeved off, Spirit. Why did you do that to me? I was really excited, I was charged up about feeling inspired and then I remembered that nothing good happens to me, so why would I bother?"

"Ego, is that a story you're carrying? That nothing good happens to you?"

"No, it's the truth."

"Every time you're confronted with thoughts that don't support your stream of inspiration, slow down and count from five down to zero – 5, 4, 3, 2, 1, 0 – and hang up! If you feel the voice of fear persisting, you can say, I'm not interested right now. Bye! Then release some anger or move your body in a way that encourages the emotion to shift. You can write down your fears and jump on them. Show them who's boss. Do you know what fear actually stands for?"

"No."

"False Emotions Appearing Real. Fear isn't even real! You can write down all your false emotions that are appearing real and destroy them. Burn them or jump all over them, get rid of them! Choose the spirit of love rather than the demon of fear."

"I can see that working for me, especially getting angry at my fearful story that I am unlovable. I'd like to burn that one and jump all over it."

"Focus on being free from fear. Imagine it now as if it's happening, just the way you would like it to be. See yourself as being completely free from fear. You've recognised that its false emotions appearing real and you've let it go. You've hung up on it and released it. You've burnt it and stomped all over it. How do you feel?"

"I feel free!"

"Go, you!"

"Okay, I can do it! I am open, willing and ready to receive freedom from fear. I'd like to connect to my universal provider now. I am Ruby Rose Taylor, 1111. All love and light now to me, all love and light now to me."

I beamed brilliantly, instantly rejoicing.

"Who is your preferred provider?"

"Who can I choose from?"

"Remember, these are only names for the divine. Names can come with preconceived ideas and therefore judgments. You may choose your own provider name. Some examples may be: the Divine, the Universe, Source Energy, Mother of Love, Kali, God, Jesus, Allah, Shiva, Buddha, Pacha Mama …" Ego interrupted with excitement,

"I'd like to try Buddha, my mother loves Buddha."

"Okay great! So, you are about to connect to Lord Buddha. Congratulations on choosing Mind Mastery. Lord Buddha is one who is fully awake. He was a human being who attained enlightenment through his own meditation practice."

"Awesome. I'm so excited to meet him."

Chapter 8

MIND MASTERY

I am Ruby Rose Taylor, 1111. I'd like to connect to Buddha consciousness now.

"Everything is an illusion, Ruby Rose."

"What?" I looked around expectantly.

"Lord Buddha? Is that you? Wow that was fast, I wasn't expecting you so quickly." He was sitting in a meditative pose under a tree. His black hair was placed in a bun on top of his head and he wore a golden yellow robe. He gestured to me to sit with him.

"It's a pleasure to meet you Ruby Rose. Let's begin with the topic of illusion. This is your biggest lesson to learn."

"Wow, you don't waste any time with small talk, do you?"

"I don't. Let's begin with the men in your life. They've all been masters of illusion."

"Well ... I don't know. I've never thought about it that way."

"Well, your biggest source of regret with the men you've been in relationship with, is that they all lied to you. Correct?"

"Yes."

"You believed the illusions they fed you. But the question is, were you really fooled or were you living in your own fantasy, projecting your reality, as you wanted it to be, on to them?"

"Woah." My head was spinning, but I began to look back through my experiences and nodded my head slowly. I was still confused by what Lord Buddha was saying, but I slowly responded.

"I know in all my relationships, I did question what was happening around me, but I never questioned things too deeply for fear that I was right."

"So, you merely touched the surface with your inquiries. You played dumb most of the time, didn't you?"

"Yes, there were times when I did question things, but then when I got the lie, I wanted, I'd go along with it."

"How did you learn this way of being?"

It suddenly clicked.

"I learnt it so I wouldn't get hurt."

"I want you to connect again. Say 'I am Ruby Rose Taylor, 1111. I am open, ready and willing to connect to Buddha consciousness'. I want you to say, 'Everything is an illusion'. See what happens and be in the presence of your experience."

"Okay, I am Ruby Rose Taylor, 1111. I would like to connect to Buddha consciousness – everything is an illusion."

My eyes involuntarily closed, and I immediately took a deep breath. Peace flooded my system, my mind instantly cleared, and it was as though I was suspended in a state of nothingness.

"If you peel back the layers of illusion that are within you and look closer at how you interact with life, you might begin to see what is really at play, "Lord Buddha continued. "In order to do this, you will need to observe life more consciously. I will teach you how to slow your thoughts and bring your mind into what's called a meditative state."

"What is a meditative state?"

"A meditative state is an experience that has the ability to transform the mind from its usual suffering. It's a technique that anyone can learn and allows you to overcome your internal limitations. It teaches you to observe the habits and patterns of your mind and, in doing so, you can become responsible for the thoughts and feelings that stop you from experiencing peace of mind.

"You can begin to acknowledge your fears and anxieties by separating them from you. You will begin to learn to observe yourself and your reactions to things. This will help you to understand the nature of life more deeply and, as you let go of old patterns of thinking, you will naturally energise your entire system through this practice of awareness."

"It sounds amazing."

"Do you interpret life through your six senses? Your eyes, ears, nose, tongue, body and mind?"

"Yes, I do."

"Well, all of it is an illusion."

"What do you mean?"

"When two people experience the same event, how can one person's experience lead to sadness and another person's to happiness?"

"Because of the way they are engaging with their senses?"

"Yes, sensory information enters your brain. It might be a picture, sound, feeling, smell or taste and, once you have interpreted it, you assign meaning to it. As soon as you give it meaning, you experience an emotion and your emotion generates your feelings, which then leads to a reaction. It tends to happen so fast that you hardly notice it as a cycle.

"Someone might say something and, before you know it, you find yourself reacting instead of witnessing the cycle. Let's try to observe this process as it occurs, so that you can train yourself to notice the cycle. Shut your eyes and sit in a comfortable position with your back straight. As you notice your mind, observe your thoughts as they present themselves. Check if these thoughts are positive or negative, healthy or toxic.

"Look at your thoughts as they come into your awareness and set a backdrop for them. This backdrop is of a river. Imagine a beautiful flowing river as you sit in meditation, observing your thoughts. Send your thoughts either to the left side of the river or the right side of it. If you experience a light thought, place it on the left side of the riverbank, and if you experience a dark thought, place it on the right side of the riverbank.

"I want you to imagine that you are sifting the silt from the river as though you are panning for gold. I'll prompt you with a thought and I want you to practise observing it as negative or positive. Do not entertain the thought and do not let it take you away from focusing on the holy river. The river is your steady flow of peace.

Your thoughts are the distractions that you are simply sifting through as you concentrate on cultivating awareness. A golden light reflects upon the river and this is illuminating your mind. Stay present.

"As you categorise each thought into toxic or healthy ones, notice if you attach a story to it. See if your mind has a habit of entertaining your thoughts, or if it will simply let go of each thought as it arises. The middle ground is the golden flow and is a state of nothingness from which you will attain freedom. Watching your thoughts helps you to see that nothing is permanent.

"You also need to observe if your thoughts are based on the future or the past. If you are thinking thoughts about the future, you can put these ahead of you, and any from the past, behind you. Try to remain centred and focused. As you get better at this practice, you will also identify when fear pops in. I'll show you an extra technique you can use to acknowledge when fear-based thinking arises."

"Thank you," I said eagerly.

"Before we get started, can I ask you a few questions about your childhood?"

"Yes, of course."

"They say a name says a lot about a person. Your name; Ruby Rose, is that light or dark?"

"Light."

"What was your upbringing like? Light or dark?"

"Hmm, light and dark! We didn't have electricity for years."

"Okay, can you tell me a little bit about it?"

"I was born in the early 1980's into an alternative family who perfected the art of home births and organic gardening. My father built our home in the seclusion of Australia's most southern island in the cold and clean landscape known as Tasmania. Have you been there?"

"I love Tasmania! Tasmania is known as the Apple Isle because so many apples are grown there. It's a sanctuary with fresh, clean air."

"Yes, exactly." I smiled with pride. He understood the beauty of my homeland. I continued. "I was born and raised in a tranquil pocket of forest in the north-west of the state called Lapoinya."

"Yes, I know it. Lapoinya is from the Aboriginal language and it means 'man ferns.'"

I looked at Lord Buddha curiously. How did he know that? Lapoinya was such a tiny place that no-one normally knew of it. I stared at him quizzically, but then I proceeded to say, "Most people don't know what a man fern is, but if you think of ferns and imagine a giant-sized one, that's basically a man fern."

"Yes, the area of Lapoinya is covered in them and there are sacred Aboriginal caves in Milabeena, not far from Lapoinya where your cousins live. In the past, the caves were used as homes for the Aboriginal tribes that migrated through the area."

"Yes!" I said awestruck. How could he possibly know that? Very few people knew about the caves; some of the locals didn't even know. I continued: "As children we also enjoyed the caves in the nearby town of Rocky Cape."

Aha! He wouldn't know that, I thought to myself, getting caught up in what was beginning to feel like a game inside my mind ...was Lord Buddha testing me?

"You were often staring in wonder at the red ochre etched on the cave walls," he said. "You have always felt a connection to indigenous cultures. I can see why you used "light" to describe your childhood. You were very free, weren't you?"

"Yes, I certainly was."

"I spent so much time in the rainforest surrounding our house when I was young, I loved it and I even turned wild! Swinging from vine to vine in the rainforest, where my home was built, I was fearless. My red hair was a fiery flame moving through the trees. We'd adventure down to the river, traipsing through the gullies and climbing down steep banks. We followed the flow of the creek till we found the rush of the river. It was a spectacular place to grow up. The sound of the river always brought us great joy. It was such a special feeling, taking that final step out of the oppressive, thick, swamp-like terrain and suddenly breaking free into the open heart of the river.

"My four sisters and I loved the feeling of the steady pull of the water around our ankles. The way across the river was precarious and uneven. Stepping on the stones would surprise us when we were launched like catapults head-first into the river. We would all start laughing together.

"As a fisherman's daughter, my sisters and I spent many moons upon the rivers of Tasmania. Many people ask me if I am called Ruby Rose because of the colour of my hair. I think my mother saw more in me than just the colour of my hair, however. I think she instinctively knew that I would be soft and gentle like a rose, but strong and determined like a ruby."

Buddha nodded his head in his all wise, knowing way as he listened attentively to my upbringing.

"The rose in you is a pure-hearted girl who wears pink-coloured glasses and sees the best in everyone."

I looked at him, moved beyond words that he understood me so well. A tear fell onto my cheek as I looked into his compassionate eyes. He could see me. I suddenly remembered my abortion and how my rose-coloured glasses had shattered inside the hospital.

"Emotions can cloud your judgement at the best of times," he said, "but you are stronger than you realise, and you can switch your perspective in any moment that you choose. Rather than dwelling on your negative point of view, why don't you focus on what it's teaching you? How has it contributed to where you are now? What are the benefits you have gained from this situation?"

I looked at him feeling angry. How could he ask me to see the good in such a bad situation? My life was ruined! I trusted him, though, and I sensed he had a deeper understanding of seeing the light in all things. He was, after all, the enlightened one.

"Well ... I didn't have healthy boundaries before, and I tried to please people all the time. I finally stood up for myself and expressed my anger."

"How can you see this situation as being an advantage to your growth and will you be taking action towards achieving above and beyond what you thought was possible before?"

"I am definitely open to seeing how this situation is a blessing in disguise. I've already promised myself that I will follow through with my dreams and that I will no longer play it safe. I'm going to listen to my heart and trust my gifts and talents from now on."

"Do you agree that your perception around abortion has completely changed?"

"I do. I have so much compassion for other women and men now. I understand their pain."

"So, from your personal experience, have you gained an idea of what it means to choose an abortion?"

"Yes, I have."

"Do you agree that your idea of abortion is based on your thoughts, feelings and emotions?"

"It is."

"Do you agree that all human beings are unique and different?"

"Yes, they are."

"Do you agree that your perception of an event will come from a state of bias, a state of personal opinion, based on your own individual experiences, thoughts and emotions?"

"Yes, it will be my own point of view and can be completely different from another's."

"Can you see how it is so individual, that you can't take anything personal?"

"Yes."

"If the guy of your dreams doesn't see you as his future wife, this has nothing to do with you. He has his own personality to deal with – his patterns, beliefs, needs, desires and his own story about what he thinks life should look like."

"It's still hard, but I am beginning to see that now."

"Don't take it to heart, because it is a waste of your precious time and energy. Just accept it. It is what it is. Be powerful in owning your thoughts and feelings, graciously move on and focus on the river that continues to flow. Don't stagnate and build emotion around the banks of your river. It won't serve you. Try not to create a story around it; just let it be. Don't become angry and bitter. I know you are very good at doing that, but that's because you've been doing that since you were little. Remember the time when you had a fight with your mother, and you ran under the house and decided that it meant that you were unlovable?"

The memory propelled me through time and space. It was sharp and it came unexpectedly. I gasped, as I was seized by the unexpected emotion. I was crying because the pain and upset was so strong. The depth of emotion rocked me. I was in darkness and, as the memory expanded, the musty smell of rotten dog bones and old cardboard boxes filled my senses. My tiny feet touched the damp earth as I crouched down, cradling my face.

Sobbing and crying, I rocked back and forth, as tears flooded my eyes. Pain poured forth from my aching heart. My mother didn't love me. No-one did. No-one cared about me. I wasn't loved. I rocked myself backwards and forwards, feeling rejected and alone. I stayed under the house, listening to the movement of footsteps above me and the muffled sounds of voices from inside the house.

I waited under the house, until I knew my mother was worried. The day turned to dusk and I hid until she started calling my name. I didn't move until I could hear the fear in her voice. Sitting with Buddha, I started to cry. Tears of sadness and grief erupted from my body. I tried to calm down as the realisation hit me. "I've been carrying that memory of feeling that I'm unlovable my whole life!"

Lord Buddha looked at me compassionately.

"You've been wearing an invisible tattoo written on your forehead that says, 'I'm unlovable, my name is Ruby Rose and I am unlovable'."

"I'm unlovable," I said as if seeing it written for the first time in bright red ink across my forehead.

"Is it any wonder that you've been attracting situations and men in your life that have proved your deepest core wounding, right?"

"What do you mean?"

"If you believe on a subconscious level that you are unlovable, and you created that belief when you were young, do you think believing it to be true has been a good thing?"

"No! It's a terrible thing. I know I've always struggled with self-love and seeing myself the way others do, but I never knew where it came from."

"Can you see how it has played out in your life?"

"Yes, I've always been afraid of rejection, I've never been able to let a guy know when I like him because I'm too afraid that I'm unlovable."

"And how have your relationships been?"

"On some levels, they've been great, but I've always discovered, at the end, lies and hidden truths. This has always left me questioning their love for me."

"You attach a story about what it means about you every time a relationship ends?"

"Yes! I make it mean that I'm responsible because the relationship failed. I blame myself and make myself wrong, like the time when I was little, and I wanted to find a way to stop my parents fighting. I blamed myself."

"You will do anything to sacrifice yourself, if it means solving the problem."

"Yes."

"Let's go back to the meditation practice I started earlier. It will help you stop making stories and attaching unnecessary emotions to everything. Do you agree that you are made up of earth, water, heat and wind?

"Earth, water, heat and wind?"

"Yes, and that your mind is a combination of sensation, perception, conception and consciousness?"

"Yes, I do."

"Do you agree that your physical body and all things in nature are in a cycle of formation, duration, deterioration and cessation? That everything is a cycle. Something is born, it lives, it breaks down and it dies."

"Yes."

"Can you apply this to your old patterns and programs that no longer serve you?"

"Yes. Everything is a cycle. It lives and it dies."

"I want you to practise observing your individual thoughts again. To start your practice, say; I am Ruby Rose Taylor, 1111, and I am connecting to Buddha Consciousness now."

"I am Ruby Rose Taylor, 1111, and I am connecting to Buddha Consciousness now."

"Picture the river of acceptance and remember light thoughts go to the left and dark thoughts to the right. Put future thoughts in front of you and any from the past, behind you."

"Okay."

"Talk me through your thoughts as they come up, so I can help you with this process and step you through it."

"A light thought has entered my mind reminding me to sit up straight."

"Place that thought to the left side of the river and let go of it. Observe it re-joining the river and flowing away."

"A light thought has entered and is about listening to the rain and being present to the sounds and sensations that I am experiencing around me."

"Great, you are very centred."

"A dark thought has entered, it's a bit murky and hasn't quite formed, but it's something to do with a guy from my past."

"Let it go and watch it re-join the river, let it float away."

"It's gone now."

"Imagine sifting through the river, panning for gold. You can stay on the top or go deeper to pan for thoughts that need to be brought to the surface. I want you to explore what happens when you get stuck on a thought and attach a story to it. I want you to experience the cycle of emotions and where the mind and body takes you. Choose a thought that is emotionally charged for you and observe where you habitually go with it."

"Sam has popped into my mind. I'm feeling angry now."

"Can you let that thought go?"

"I'm stuck on it."

"This is something we can explore together. Sit with your anger and feel it, so we can see the story that you have attached to it."

"I'm feeling angry with Sam because I don't think he loves me; I think he played a game and it meant nothing."

"Go deeper again, sifting through the river, exploring what's there for you?"

"I feel sad."

"Why?"

"I miss our connection. But I can't speak to him anymore, because he never really loved me."

"You're very strong and determined, aren't you?"

"I guess I am."

"Can you see that you have interpreted what happened and made it mean something?"

"I've made it mean that because he didn't choose to be with me, that he doesn't care about me."

"But, if you reflect on the time that you shared, did you enjoy your experience with him?"

"We had a wonderful time together."

"Was it a special connection for you?"

"It was very deep for me."

"Did you experience feelings of love?"

"I did."

"Did you enjoy those feelings?"

"Very much."

"Go within yourself now. Do you really believe that he didn't love you?"

"He did love me! I did experience the magic of love with him and his actions were very caring during the time we were together. He cared deeply for me and now I can see that I've created an ugly story, because I've interpreted what happened at the end and made it mean it was terrible."

"Do you have a habit of thinking the worst and finding it hard to believe that you are lovable?"

"Oh, my goodness, yes!" I started to feel a deep surge of emotion inside me as hot tears streamed down my face. The stagnation within me began to release. I let go of the story, I was holding on to."

"What is really there for you?"

"Loss. I miss our connection, our intimacy and the fun we used to have together."

"That sounds like attachment to me."

"It is."

"Can you focus your connection on others? Focus on your loving feelings for others for a moment."

"Yes, I can feel it with my family, my sisters, my cousins, my friends, innocent children and strangers in the street."

"What is inside that connection?"

"A beautiful feeling of love."

"When you focus on love, do you feel the attachment to Sam?"

"No."

"Do you feel at peace with the situation?"

"I feel happy that I have moved on and that everything has unfolded the way it has."

"You are no longer clinging on to anything?"

"I feel unconditional love for everyone and everything."

Can you let go of your old story with Sam now?"

"It feels easy to let go."

"Watch it go now, that old story. Watch your new story with positive thoughts flowing by, too. Let everything go and watch it flow down the river. Bring your focus back to the peaceful flow of the river. How do you feel?"

"Like I've been holding onto something that's been destroying me and, now that I've released it, it feels like a weight has shifted inside me. Seeing the river running through me feels healing and freeing. I didn't even realise that I was making it into a story. I thought I was feeling angry because he hurt me, but when I looked closely at the truth, I could see that I'm not really looking at the situation clearly because I'm holding on to the need to be wounded.

I'm finding a reason to suffer when, in fact, I'm free. I don't have to stay in the prison of my own thoughts anymore. I'm judging him and making him wrong. I've been criticising him and that isn't making me feel very good, because I want to feel love. Judging him is making me feel worse and keeping me trapped in the past.

"I didn't even realise I was carrying so much emotion. It's like I've been blocking what is there. Thank you for showing me how to let go of the past so I can be more present."

"You can do this every day, training yourself to powerfully observe your mind and emotional body. It's so important to give yourself this time every day to check in and clear any stagnant thoughts that are lurking around. Once you become proficient at meditating, then you can purposefully choose your thoughts and increase your conscious ability to attract positive situations into your life."

"Wow! That sounds amazing, I really want to get good at this. Some days when my thoughts get bad, I can't wait for the day to be over. I want to disappear from my mind."

"It sounds like what you are really saying is, you wish you could disappear from yourself?"

"Yes, exactly. I want all my thoughts to disappear, so that I can slip into the stillness of the night."

"Are there days when you feel it start to happen, but you notice it and can stop it?"

"Some days I can stop it, but there are times when I don't even realise that my thoughts are taking me wherever they want to go. I want to choose my thoughts consciously."

"You will, Ruby. It can be as simple as asking yourself this question, 'Am I choosing this or is it choosing me?' If you start every day with mindfulness, you will become powerful very quickly. Have you ever made breakfast, sat down and eaten it?"

"Of course!"

"How many times have you switched over to autopilot and been so caught up in the noise of your mind, that you aren't present while eating your food?"

"It happens all the time."

"As part of your daily awareness practice, I'd like you to include making yourself a cup of tea. There is a ceremonial art to making and drinking tea that we practise. You can learn that later, but for now at the end of your meditation practise have a cup of your favourite tea beside you and, when you've finished meditating, try to drink your tea in complete mindfulness. Focus on the sensations, the smell, the taste and the texture.

"Being less busy in your mind opens the door to observing, looking, noticing, watching, seeing, hearing and smelling. This leads to presence and clarity. When you are grounded in this way, you can direct your thoughts consciously and literally choose what you want to think and feel."

Chapter 9

CHILDHOOD BELIEFS

I nodded at Lord Buddha as he continued his lesson.

"Why do you think it is easier to choose a negative thought when it makes you feel sick to your stomach, stressed out and anxious, than a nurturing thought that feeds your entire system with light?"

Lord Buddha was testing me on my habitual patterns.

"It's a really good question. Perhaps I am in the habit of holding on to pain, instead of letting it go."

"Why don't you maintain focus on thoughts that provide support for your wellbeing?"

"Perhaps it's self-sabotage? A lack of self-esteem? Not taking care of myself and what I'm thinking?"

"Have you ever noticed how your body reacts when you think positive thoughts?"

"My body thrives on positivity. I feel fantastic when I'm thinking powerful thoughts."

"Try this and notice what happens to your mind and body. Sit with yourself comfortably and take a slow deep breath. Tell yourself:

I'm safe and it's over.

"Try this negative one to compare:

I'm not safe and there's danger everywhere.

"Switch between the two until you really notice the difference."

"I feel so relieved when I say,' I'm safe and it's over'. Thank you. It is over, I can let it go now."

"Did you know that I travelled throughout India with my disciples, teaching and spreading spiritual growth to people for 45 years until I died at the age of 80?"

"I didn't realise you spent 45 years teaching. You have a very big heart to spend your whole life committed to helping others."

"I knew my brothers and sisters were suffering. I felt compelled to help them, so I created Vipassana – a place where people can go and gain awareness of the inner workings of their mind. It gives people an opportunity to watch and notice their mind. You explore reality and, with practice, you can break through illusion and find yourself in the presence of light. You will experience a transformation when you reach this state. I call it liberation. It is permanent and is the goal of meditation."

"How did you learn it?"

"For many years I was unaware, like you. I grew up very sheltered, below the Himalayan foothills in a small kingdom in northern India, called Nepal. My father was very protective and kept me in the confines of his palace, shielding me from the outside world. When I was 29 years old, I took a walk outside the palace walls and what I saw changed my life. I saw an old man suffering from ageing, disease and death. I became deeply troubled because I had not learnt about the ailments of humanity. I also saw a hermit at peace with himself, completely at ease and in the flow of life.

"I found myself compelled to understand the human condition, so I left my family and became a student, learning from teachers and trying many things in the search for eternal peace. At the age of 35, in 525 BC, I abandoned all that I knew and stayed in nature for a very long time. I meditated under a Bodhi tree under the full moon and finally broke free from my mind, gaining deeper insights into human life. As I realised the truth of the universe, I became enlightened.

"Every day the sun will rise, and the sun will set. The rivers will flow towards the ocean and, at night, the stars will illuminate an indigo sky. The Earth will tilt on its axis 23.5 degrees and rotate slowly as the seasons shift. The birds will migrate to the north and, although you might not take the time to notice, life will continue in a cycle: birth, life, death and rebirth.

Chapter 9: Childhood Beliefs

"You need to know that within this cycle there are also layers – your mental body, emotional body, physical body and spiritual body. This program teaches you to identify the layers within you. A lot of it is connected to your childhood. As a child, you were innocent, perfect, whole and complete. But once language was introduced, you started creating stories about why things happened to you.

"You drew your own conclusions and made it mean something about you, often to the detriment of your self-esteem, self-worth and confidence. When you realise that this is not true and that you have been lying to yourself, you will stop believing your stories and experience true freedom and peace for the first time in your life.

"All your negative thoughts are silly stories that you made up when you were upset. All that has happened is that you've held on to your stories you created when you were little.

"Slow down your thoughts. Your judging mind will always be louder than your true being. Acknowledge this and ask the thoughts to leave you. Tell all those voices in your head that they are not you. Anything negative about others or you isn't connected to who you really are. Within you is an endless amount of potential and your life can be filled with love, inspiration and belief. Better to focus on this, than fear, criticism or doubt. I believe you can rise above it. I believe you are brave, and you are powerful."

As you start your journey, you might experience feelings of fear about letting go of your old stories and allowing yourself to become who you really are. You might feel nervous about stepping into the unknown and uncertain about what you will find on the road ahead but, I can assure you, all you need to do is concentrate on the word 'trust'. Trust will become your life force, because trust is the vital ingredient to the story of your happiness."

"Trust?"

"Yes, trust. Focus on creating your life exactly as you want it to be. Bring your attention to all the things that make you excited, passionate and inspired."

"That's easy. I can do that!"

"Many people feel confused in life. They often describe life as hard or it's a roller coaster. They feel as if they are going up and down all the time. Do you know what I'm talking about?"

"I feel like that."

"Promise yourself that life is perfect exactly the way it is. Go to sleep every night and claim the energy of the following statement.

Life is perfect.

Every heartache, every challenge, every success.

It is all part of my journey.

I trust in life; I trust in the divine unfolding of every experience.

I trust there is a greater plan for me.

"A great way to become clear about your life and what it is that gives you a sense of purpose is to list your top five passions. What are you passionate about?"

"I love creativity; it's my absolute favourite thing. I love singing, dancing, painting, writing and playing. I'm so happy when I do anything creative because It makes me feel connected."

"What is your second passion?"

"Physical exercise. Moving my body puts me into a peak state of mind. I love to run, bike ride, rock climb, salsa dance, practise yoga, make time for meditation and play football. I love any type of physical exercise because it makes me feel so good."

"I'm so pleased to hear that."

"My third passion is healthy living. When I'm treating my body well, I feel so good about myself. I love eating whole foods, especially locally grown organic produce from the farmers markets. I love making cold-pressed vegetable juices and drinking spring water. It makes me feel cleansed, light and clear."

"Yes, I agree with you."

"My fourth passion is being around people. I love spending quality time with my friends and family. It helps me feel connected and supported."

"Your fifth passion?"

"Being in nature. I love the outdoors and travelling to new places. I come alive with the feeling of adventure and I find nature grounding and calming."

"Your passions will lead you in the direction of fulfilling your life purpose. Are you currently working in a creative field and using your gifts and talents?"

"No, I'm working as a primary school teacher."

"Do you feel fulfilled?"

"I love children, but the truth is I feel like something is missing in my life."

"What is it that you long to do?"

"Create, sing and write."

"What's stopping you?"

"I'm scared of going out on my own, I guess."

Lord Buddha looked deep into my eyes and didn't say a word. I began to feel confronted; it was as though he could see my thought patterns, my core beliefs and even my inner battles. It was as though he knew my mind, better than I did.

"Look over there, far away into the distance," he said. "Can you see that the sun is filling the horizon with the promise of something slightly mysterious near those misty mountains?"

"It looks like an adventure waiting to happen."

"Allow the golden hues of liberation to cast themselves upon you. Let your mind become still. What vision lights your way? What words are whispering to you as you enter into a higher state?"

"I can hear myself say, 'believe in yourself'."

"What do you see?"

"I can see an onion with a beam of light peeling through my internal layers. One layer says, 'patterns picked up from my mother and father', another says, 'patterns I picked up from my lineage', the next says 'patterns from the human collective' and another says, 'patterns from past lives'. Everything is spinning and I'm seeing a bright light."

"That indicates you're ready for an upgrade in the program. Well done. You have successfully awakened!"

A deep voice broke through the intimate space I was sharing with Lord Buddha.

"You are now ready to explore your subconscious mind. If you are willing to enter this next stage of the program, simply say 'Yes' and we'll transfer you to the next phase of Spiritual Spring."

Feeling quite surprised at how quickly everything was progressing, I asked the question.

"Is that it, Lord Buddha?"

"You have seen beyond illusion. You are ready. You are never alone because there is no separation. You can connect to me anytime you choose."

"Oh, well in that case then, Yes, I am ready for the next phase of self-realisation." I turned to Lord Buddha and said.

"I really appreciate the time you've taken to teach me about meditation and for helping me to become more present. I know it will help me to be free from my habit of creating stories."

"You certainly have the tools to experience lasting peace and fulfilment, I wish you all the best on your path to enlightenment."

"Thank you so much!"

I gave Lord Buddha a hug and squeezed him so tight that he started to laugh. I was feeling so grateful for all that he had taught me.

"Goodbye for now, Ruby Rose."

"Goodbye, Lord Buddha."

Chapter 10

A TEST

I felt elated as a sudden urge to stampede forwards with vigour and strength overcame me. I was on to the next stage of the program! Yes! I picked up a red flag and began waving it at anyone who would listen to my newfound knowledge.

"I made it through! I've got it all figured out! There's nothing to fear because it's all an illusion! It's all a story and it's not even real! Life is great and it's actually easy!"

A loud voice broke through my excitement.

"It looks like you're ready for your next lesson."

"What?" I stuttered, as I instinctively sensed a challenge coming my way.

"It's time for an upgrade."

Fear and doubt began marching toward me like two well-built marine soldiers. My mind clouded over and I began to second-guess my ability to progress in the program.

"I'm not sure I have what it takes," I mumbled out loud. "I mean, I've only just begun to understand that I've been creating stories my whole life. Can't I have some time to absorb it first?"

I was sensing with intuitive dread that my joyful jubilation was about to come crashing down.

In one swift swoop the world I was in began to dissolve and disappear. I watched in horror as the mountainous landscape bubbled and rippled as everything crumbled, crushed and disintegrated around me. It was as if I were in a virtual reality video game. I began to feel vulnerable and miserable.

"What's happening?"

A dust storm began circling around me as I cried out. "Why is this happening?"

I was feeling confused. Everything was hazy and my mind cloudy.

"Now I can't even think properly."

I started to cry as I began to feel angry and overwhelmed by the sudden change. Strong feelings of being out of my comfort zone began to overwhelm me."

"Why me?" I pleaded. "I thought I had it all figured out. Now I'm lost again."

I wiped my tear-stained face with a handkerchief, feeling very sorry for myself.

"Batter up! Now you are ready for the game." the Universe bellowed enthusiastically, enjoying this stage of the program the most. Nodding my head sadly, I obediently did as I was told. I began cursing myself for advancing to the next level of the program.

"Why do I always say 'Yes' before thinking it through?"

"Because you're a thrill-seeker. We like that about you. You have an open mind and you're willing to go for things."

"Thanks," I grumbled unhappily.

The dust had begun to settle, and I found myself on the perimeter of a large oval. I strode gallantly onto the field with the grime from the dust still stuck in my eyes.

I walked onto the cricket pitch; I knew where to stand because I'd played cricket as a kid.

Picking up the bat lying before the wickets, I did my best to stand as ready as I could. People in the grandstands were cheering me on.

"You can do it!" I heard them yelling. For some reason they were eager to watch me play. I put my game face on, and I jumped up and down psyching myself up. I did a quick scan of the crowd and tried to make out who my supporters were. Someone was waving to me, dressed in white, but I couldn't quite see because the sun was shining into my eyes.

Chapter 10: A Test

I took my place as confidently as I could at the crease. The Great Creator bowled me one down the pitch. I saw the ball hurtling toward me. Oh no! It was a spinner heading straight for my pearly whites and it was coming down the line towards me at a rapid speed.

I stepped to the side, feeling afraid. I thought I was going to get knocked in the mouth but, at the last minute, the ball spun toward my wicket and smashed straight through my stumps. My innings was over! I was out for a duck! The crowd sighed with disappointment.

"You're unlovable!" they all shouted as they turned their backs on me. I began to cry. My deepest wounding began to resurface, the landscape shifted, and I was swept up in a tsunami of emotions as a great wave of insecure thoughts and feelings started dumping me.

"You're unlovable, nobody loves you; you're a nobody!"

I tried to stay calm as the waves gathered speed around me, but all my sensitivities were being triggered now. I wanted to swim for safety, my heart was racing, and I felt panicky.

"I'm unlovable," I moaned.

"It's true." My past began floating toward me on a surfboard and I began to feel overwhelmed. Three disastrous relationships with men! My first boyfriend was appearing before my eyes and was moving towards me. He had aged quite a bit from the handsome Australian with blonde hair I used to know as a 16-year-old. The ugliness of his betrayal poured forth from his heart in a swirl of dark energy and lies. Aghhh it hurts, aghhh! He looked at me begging forgiveness, as all the women he'd slept with came forward. Their eyes filled with sadness as their shame shrouded their hearts. Some of them were my closest friends! I felt a sharp stab in the back from my boyfriend's best mate as he came from behind me. I screamed at him.

"I thought I could trust you! I thought you were my friend!"

When my boyfriend started sleeping with his girlfriend, he had taken revenge and revealed to me nine years of their dirty secrets, including the times my boyfriend had sex with a prostitute. The shock of it all and not knowing who to trust had deeply damaged my sense of safety and security.

"Leave me alone!" I shrieked.

My wish was heard, and they all vanished. But then my manipulative second boyfriend came out of nowhere. Oh, no, please! The torture of being with Aiden was too much to bear. He had destroyed me! Please! Get him away from me! He's a narcissistic sociopath! I took years to recover from the damage of being with Aiden! Get him away from me!"

Suddenly, now Sam was swimming towards me. Oh, my goodness! I saw, with crystal-clear clarity, the pattern I was repeating. I was involved with men who never honoured me in monogamy. Where did this pattern come from? I suddenly knew. My mother and father had never been in a monogamous relationship either! I was awake to something that might be cleared! My fears, saboteurs and subconscious beliefs from these experiences were bobbing around me as messages of "I'm not worthy to receive love!"

I desperately searched for a rescuer. Can't someone save me? "Where's the life raft?" I called to the heavens. "How can I stop this pattern with men?"

The deafening tone of emptiness was the response I received.

"Thanks for nothing, Universe," I grumbled, dissatisfied with my half-eaten piece of humble pie.

I tried to find something to cling on to. Was there anything stable to help me settle my thoughts and feelings? I became highly sensitive to the mishaps and challenges of my life.

"Why does this keep happening to me?" I moaned. "When am I ever going to experience true love?"

I began slipping into a "poor me" dialogue with my victim self, muttering and mumbling about the curses in my life.

"I think I have everything figured out and then along comes a challenge that knocks me off my feet. Or, is that part of what they are teaching me?"

I stopped my self-piteous act when I saw something in the water.

"What's that?" I was suddenly full of energy, swimming with vigour and strength towards a wooden raft that was floating quietly on the misty river. Made from tea-tree logs, it reminded me of a raft

I'd made in scouts when I was only 10 years old. As I touched the logs and clung to the raft, I felt a flood of relief calming me. I was safe. I was going to be okay. I let my breath settle. Calm feelings began to sink in as I realised, I was through the worst of it.

"You always get through everything that life throws at you," the Universe said, as I pulled myself up to the safety of the raft, my clothes heavy and dripping. I managed to drag my tired body onto it.

Breathing heavily, I slowly arrived into a place of trust. I began to see with 20-20 vision that the Universe had just bowled me a blessing in disguise. If that didn't happen, I wouldn't have seen the pattern. Why is hindsight always 20-20 after the fact?"

"Because we want you to learn to trust in everything and learn the art of surrender," the Universe said.

"Is that how I grow? Trusting that a nightmare is really a dream? That all my relationships have actually been blessings?"

"Yes."

"When I'm being challenged in the program and have to face the unknown, are you training me?"

"Your resilience is being tested. We want to observe how well you face adversity and if you can trust that the process is unfolding according to a greater plan. We want to know if you will survive or thrive."

"The sunflowers! Okay, Universe! I'm ready for my next innings. Now, I know I can survive."

I reflected on the sudden catastrophe they had dumped on me. It had come out of nowhere. As I sat there drifting on the smoky water and the initial shock of the event began to abate, I was able to peer inside the fabric of my life and ask a question burning deep within me.

"So, what is it all about then, this great mystery of life?"

A dark cloak was lying on the raft.

"That wasn't there before?" I said to myself as I knelt toward it and felt the soft texture of the velvet. I began to feel curious.

"Take a look inside," the Universe replied.

I wasn't a hundred percent sure I was ready to find out what was inside the cloak but, with courage in my heart, I peered inside the surrounding darkness. A rich smell entered my nostrils and I asked again,

"Why are you so mysterious? I can feel and sense you but, when you are cloaked in darkness, I can't make out who you are."

"I am your subconscious mind," a voice answered quietly. Looking around, as though the voice had come from somewhere else, a feeling of intrigue and a spark of excitement came over me. My subconscious mind spoke again.

"You are about to uncover the great mystery of what it means to be human."

"Oh, my goodness! This is a dream come true! Tell me everything!" I was feeling very blessed.

"Thank you, Universe, I love you!" I turned towards the black cloak and asked the question burning on my lips.

"Can you help me to understand what my abortion is really about and what I'm meant to be learning?"

"Yes, I can tell you the root cause of your deepest issues. The root cause of your issue is low self-esteem. You've taken this journey to heal your subconscious beliefs and create new and empowering stories about yourself.

"Ok," I said eagerly, keen to know more."

"You're going through a spiritual cycle of birth, life, death and rebirth. It's all you need to know.

"Will it be a happy ending?"

"The happy ending is the rebirth phase. When you begin to integrate your experiences and lessons from your life and death phase, this prepares you for the birth and expansion of something new. It could be a new relationship, a new career, a new life or spiritual growth."

"But don't fixate on a happy ending, remember everything is impermanent and leads you to the next cycle of growth."

"Ok, thank you."

Chapter 10: A Test

"By now Ruby Rose, I'm sure you have learnt that reaching happiness is not a destination. If you raise your vibration and commit to a daily practice of meditation, you will experience joy every day, but it comes from within, not from meeting the perfect guy or having your dream car."

"Yes, I have learnt that it is the journey that counts and the experiences along the path to reaching my dreams are just as rich as the final destination."

"You are on a journey and life is your mysterious teacher, prodding you to keep following your heart and stay true to yourself."

Chapter 11

BUYING HAPPINESS

"Take a look inside the fabric of my cloak."
"Ok sure."
"There are things you need to see."
"I'm ready!"
"You will need to look past your illusions – past your perceptions and your beliefs. After some time, you will see sparkly diamonds."
"Sparkly diamonds? How incredible!"
"You'll need to look deeply into the darkness and shine your light on what no longer serves you."
"Ok Sub-con, I am willing to look at my shadows and let go, I will do whatever it takes!"
"In order to grow, you must be able to overcome and welcome challenges."
"I welcome all challenges with grace and ease."
"Good! Let's get started! From a young age, you have been conditioned to survive in a society that subconsciously teaches you to buy 'happiness' from images flashing hypnotically on your screens."
"Oh, my gosh you are right!"
"You are susceptible to subliminal messages."
"I am highly suggestible and I find it hard to say no."
"Watching these images in your most impressionable years has trained you to focus your attention on a state of lack."
"A state of lack?"

"Yes, I will explain why. Imagine you are raising a child and she is watching an advertisement on her device. She sees a young girl, exactly like herself, playing with the latest Barbie doll and she announces to you, her mother, 'I want that mermaid Barbie, too!'

"You plan to buy it for her birthday. Or, if she persists, you will find a way to give it to her sooner. Instead of experiencing joy from within, your daughter learns to look outside of herself to find fulfilment."

"Oh, is that what you mean?"

"Yes! Now think about this. If advertisements were telling you that you are loved and you are special exactly as you are, there would be no reason to sell you anything. So, who is persuading who? Is it your sense of worth or your fear of inadequacy that is driving your decisions? Are you being influenced by a constant flow of media and advertisements?"

"I am when I am watching television."

"Do you succumb to instant gratification or can you delay it?"

"I try to be as minimal as possible and not get caught up in consumerism."

"Check to see that your true self is guiding you and not the commercialised agenda of social media around you."

"My true self? What do you mean?"

"Your connection to who you really are. Your all-knowing self."

"My true self wants to spend time in nature and play music!"

"The economy doesn't care that you want to spend time in nature and make music. It cares whether you spend money or not. Attempting to find happiness inside a marketing strategy aimed at taking your money is going to be short lived."

"I totally agree Sub-con!"

"They are suggesting to you that when you want something, you should buy it, even if you can't afford it and don't have the money. They even offer to lend you the money! They claim it will make you happy, but it doesn't! Try something for a moment Ruby. Repeat after me."

I felt stirred by the voice speaking such prophetic wisdom. In awe, I nodded my head and as I did, I saw two small lights inside the coat beginning to twinkle at me.

"I see the lights!"

"You are in a highly suggestible state. Please repeat this. We need to reprogram your subconscious mind."

Subconscious mind, I want you to hear with every part of you this truth that I am acceptable, and I am enough. All the pain, the insecurity, the lifelong suffering from low self-esteem is transforming today.

Today is a new day and I will be shifting from being a victim and shifting into a state of empowerment. I will no longer play the role of being a servant. I am not here to look after everyone. I am becoming an Empress unto myself and my needs are important.

I serve myself with love and nourishment. I stop being a martyr and sacrificing myself all the time for the sake of others. I am becoming a warrior as I step up to honour myself.

Now, I am an empowered and courageous truth-seeker stepping forward with vigour and strength. I am no longer a pretender; I am a lover. I release my overly intellectual side and I open to my intuition. I release my need to be an egotist and now embrace my higher self.

A wave of emotion hit me as I said the statement aloud. Deep in the core of my being, my stomach began to shudder as feelings of deep inadequacy began to release from within me. Tears blurred my vision and I cradled my head in my hands.

Wow, this is deep work. I could feel the hope in my heart growing and I breathed with relief as I said the words:

I am totally acceptable as I am. I am enough.

Mr. Sub-con encouraged me with more, so I continued as directed.

All negative behaviours are leaving me today. I step into a new pair of shoes, a new spirit, a clean mind and a refreshed body. It is safe for me to do this; I am enough, and I am loved. Every cell and every part of me, right down to my soul, is safe.

It's over. I am opening the door to a world that will forever awaken my true birthright. Filled with unconditional love for myself, light, joy and freedom fill my

Spiritual Spring

heart. I will live life in my heart. All anger, hate and feelings that "I'm not lovable" clear away.

I am free, it is my time to shine bright. It is my time to shine because I am a child of the universe and I am loved.

"Wow! This is amazing. I feel great."

"Mastering your subconscious mind is a life-changing process. It's a bit like being stuck inside a cage that you don't even know you're stuck inside. Suddenly someone hands you a golden key to help you access your inner freedom.

"I love it Mr. Sub-con, I feel so powerful now!"

"Your next download will give you a new way of being. Are you ready to open the door?"

"I hope so."

"You can do it!"

"Yes, I can! I want to be free!"

Chapter 12

ALTERING STATES

Mr. Sub-con handed me a golden key and I placed it carefully inside the lock. I turned it curiously. The door opened and, I saw a laser beam light up the words: Mind Mastery.

A voice spoke from the darkness inside the room.

"Welcome to the next stage of the program. You are now entering Mind Mastery."

Eleven enticing letters blinked encouragingly at me, beckoning me to explore.

"Do you want to see the sparkly diamonds again?"

"Yes, please."

"Activate the button." Mr. Sub-con said.

I pressed the button down enthusiastically and the download for my program began booting up. My mind cleared, my thoughts slowed, and an enlightened sense of perspective started filling me with calm confidence.

Sub-con spoke softly. "You will be shown the core beliefs that are holding you hostage and limiting your self-belief. But, before you can access your repressed memories, you need to understand the different states of consciousness. Are you ready?"

"Yes, I am."

"Here we go. In the first seven years of your life, you were operating in what's called a Theta state. There are four building blocks of consciousness, otherwise known as states of awareness that are categorised by different brainwave patterns and frequencies. They are measured in Hz or cycles per second. The slower the frequency, the more relaxed you feel.

Beta is the state of being alert, focused and active. Images, sensations and mental processes are dominant in this brainwave. When you over-think and worry too much, you will benefit from altering your state and lowering your brainwaves. You can slow your brainwaves down by breathing, relaxing and day-dreaming your way into the alpha setting.

When you are in Alpha, your brainwaves are between 8 and 13 Hz. This frequency is a bridge between the conscious and the Subconscious. As you are drifting off to sleep and right before you wake up, you are transitioning between Alpha and Theta.

As you are cycling down from Alpha to Theta, be sure to program how you want to feel and even what you want to achieve the next day. You are highly suggestible in this state, so steer your thoughts to positive things and you will wake up feeling the same as when you went to sleep."

"Is that why when I go to bed worrying about something, I wake up feeling anxious?"

"Yes. It is so important to meditate and pray for 15 minutes as you are going to sleep every night. To help transmute negative energy you can visualise the violet ray of Saint Germain. This ray dissolves negative energy. Then, imagine a pillar of white light encapsulating the purple ray. Place your hands on your heart and breathe in golden light and say, 'I am opening the door to my heart. I welcome the prince of peace who loves and cares for me. I welcome heart consciousness and I invite you into my heart. I am ready to connect to the almighty presence of love. I am open, willing and ready to receive all love and all light now. I am Ruby Rose Taylor, 1111, and I am ready to connect to the source of love within me. I am the love and I am the light'."

"If you do this every morning and night, I can guarantee you will feel deeply connected to yourself and at peace. Always make sure you are programming yourself for success."

"I like the sound of that."

"You can speak directly to me and tell me what you want. You can choose how you're going to feel and create what you want in life by your thoughts and feelings. If it is jump out of bed and do a happy dance, I will listen, and I will remind you to do it. I am very obedient when you demand things of me."

"This is my chance to be bossy!"

"Yes, exactly!"

The next state you need to learn about is Theta. In this cycle, your brainwaves are between 4 and 8 Hz and you experienced life in this frequency in your early years. During your childhood, you absorbed and interpreted ideas, beliefs and thoughts about yourself and everything around you. You recorded what your parents said about you and even what they felt about themselves. Everything that happened, even your birth and your experiences inside the womb, can be accessed via hypnosis once you are in a Theta state. Every experience is recorded. You might not consciously remember it, but your subconscious does."

"Well, aren't you amazing?" I said as Mr. Sub-con beamed,

"Yes, I am, but I can be quite limiting if I don't have the right programming. Most of my beliefs were created as a child trying to make sense of the world. It's important to reboot the system of limiting beliefs in your adult years. Higher states of consciousness, hypnosis and spiritual experiences occur in the Theta cycle, too. It is here that repressed memories and emotions are accessed. By applying certain techniques such as staring and using "deepeners" it becomes possible to enter a theta state of one's own accord."

"You mean, I can do it myself?"

"I am going to teach you how to take yourself into a Theta state and speak to me directly whenever you need to."

"Wow! That is so cool!"

"Be sure to activate your all-knowing self as you take yourself down into Theta."

"How?"

"Simply state your intention."

I always choose to enter a deep state with my true self leading the journey.

"Okay, it sounds easy enough."

"Your next state to learn about is Delta. Are you writing notes?"

"Yes, I remember much better when I write things down."

"Ok, so in the Delta cycle, your brainwaves slow to 4 Hz. This is your deep sleep state and is described by noted psychologist Carl Jung as the 'collective unconscious'."

"The collective unconscious? What does that mean?"

"The collective includes everyone on the planet. When we talk about the level of fear that the collective is carrying, we are talking about humanity as a whole – how fear is affecting us as a species and what it looks like."

"What does it look like?"

"It looks like; suffering. This program is shifting the vibration on the planet."

"Woah, that sounds way bigger than I can grasp right now."

"It is, but you are an important part of this mission. We have chosen you to lead the way. But first you need to clear your energy and shift your vibration before you can help others in the collective."

"Oh, my goodness! You think I can do that? How on earth will I be able to help others?"

"You will find that in healing yourself, you will naturally heal others, too."

"You might be interested to know that neurologists have now introduced a fifth state of consciousness that they're now calling the gamma brainwave."

"Okay, let me write that down."

"Studies have shown that this cycle measures an expanded awareness of spiritual consciousness, and researchers have been observing it in individuals like Tibetan Buddhist monks. This is where you come in, Ruby Rose. We are working towards expanding your spiritual consciousness."

"What on earth do you mean? I know nothing about this."

"Yes, but you are here nonetheless."

"Well, if those Tibetan monks are anything like the Lord Buddha, then it's no wonder they have an expanded awareness."

"Yes, exactly. The work you did with Lord Buddha was great and I want to expand on what he was teaching you."

"Sure."

"If you created a belief about yourself in the first seven years of your life that said, I'm not lovable, then unfortunately you're going to find a reason to make that true."

"How come?"

"What you think and feel about yourself, is so powerful that it will manifest into physical form. You will not feel good enough to follow that dream, not good enough to change careers and not smart enough to even attempt it.

"You will convince yourself that 'I'm not intelligent enough' and you might even believe that 'I don't deserve to be seen and heard, so what's the point anyway? I don't matter'. The good news is that all of these core beliefs can be reprogrammed into powerful mantra."

"Mantra?"

"Yes, mantra are sacred messages that carry psychological and spiritual powers. The mind is very suggestive and all you must do is repeat these powerful messages over and over again. Gradually over time, as you consistently practise these mantras, you will actually form new neural pathways in the brain. You will experience ecstatic bliss from practising mantras. It gives you an opportunity to connect to your true self."

"My true self? You mentioned it before, but I don't really understand what it is."

"Your true self is the awareness within you that you are a divine being capable of shifting your consciousness from ego consciousness to cosmic consciousness. But first, learn to connect to yourself in a state of conscious awareness, because you need to see all the different parts of yourself that are not who you really are.

"Through this process of awareness, you can clear old patterns of thinking that have become stuck over time. You will become aware of your inner critic and any negative beliefs that make you feel separate from loving yourself. The key is to speak directly to the part of yourself that is negative. Speak to the inner critic with powerful mantra that stems from awareness of the truth of who you really are."

"That sounds really fun, but I have no idea what it looks like."

"Come over here."

I followed Mr. Sub-con to a row of blinking lights and saw the buttons: Beta, Alpha, Theta, Delta and Gamma.

"Hit the button that says Theta. This is the best brainwave to reset your core beliefs because this relaxed state will help you focus. If you want to transform your limiting beliefs, I suggest you do it now."

I hit the button eagerly and Mr. Sub-con's voice slowed down and softened.

"Today in this session, Ruby Rose, you will uncover a part of you known as the inner critic. Your inner critic is standing in your way. In this deep state, as your brainwaves slow, you will have the opportunity to clear negative energy in the form of thoughts and feelings from your mental, physical and emotional body."

"That sounds amazing, Mr. Sub-con. Thank you."

"I'd like you to lie back on the table." Mr. Sub-con gestured to a table with white sheets. I hopped on to the table and got comfortable."

"I want you to find a spot on the ceiling above you to focus on. Stare at that spot with laser beam intensity and put your full awareness on it.

"Take a nice, deep breath in and let all the tension in your body go. The deeper you go, the better you feel and the better you feel, the deeper you go. Dropping all the way down now, further down than you have ever gone before, you drop into complete relaxation. Invite your mind, body, heart and spirit to join as one in this meditation, so that you can become fully centered and present on setting your intention.

"Set your intention now to come into full awareness. There is nothing you need to do here and there is nothing asked of you. This is your time to connect. Feel deeply into your body as you connect with your true self. Send your body acknowledgement for the work that goes unnoticed.

"Acknowledge the pathways that are running throughout your system; your immune, adrenal, lymphatic, respiratory, reproductive, excretory and endocrine system. Gently nod your head and say,

I acknowledge my body. My body is a miracle. I am an intelligent being with multiple systems supporting me.

"Bring liberation to your mind now. Thank your mind for being with you in this session, give your mind permission to be completely at ease.

Thank you, mind for being with me in this session, I give you permission to be completely at ease. To be here now, free from thoughts and free from attachments.

"Give your mind permission to become completely spacious and open."

I did as Mr. Sub-con suggested and felt myself opening to stillness.

I could feel deep peace settling inside my mind, holding me still, holding me within the beat of my heart and the pulse of energy that was making its way all around my body.

I could see shooting stars of light, circulating energy, life force and vitality throughout my entire system, through my brain, through my beating heart and into my lungs.

The movement of energy was expanding my spine, my structure and lifting me upwards. Supporting me to become tall and broad.

Mr. Sub-con commanded me to repeat a statement:

I am safe to completely let go.

A beautiful sense of ease and comfort began spreading through my stomach, clearing out stagnant energy as it went – rinsing, washing and releasing.

"Visualise all emotion dissipating now with the violet flame. All darkness is being turned into light, soothing the bowels, nourishing the intestines. Generating love – unconditional love. Creating non-attachment to outcomes or expectations. Repeat this,

I am present to the acceptance of all that is. I am present to the perfection of my true self.

"Drop further down, all the way down and let your breath flow through your body. Every sensation helps you to drop deeper now and you are being nourished by tranquil peace and harmony. Open into your hips, expand beyond your limitations and invite any negative core beliefs to be released throughout this session.

"As you focus on this, bring your life force further down into your thighs, spread love throughout your body and witness sparkles of light running along your meridian lines. Vessels, tissues and capillaries are working together to create harmony now in your body, mind and heart. Say this now:

I am becoming whole and connected. Deeply, peacefully and calmly. I am letting go, deeply, peacefully, and calmly. I am dropping down and down. Dropping into my thighs and my knees.

Any unresolved issues from my childhood are invited to be released and cleansed. Through awareness of my heart, I am in a state of love, acceptance, peace and forgiveness.

Dropping down deeper now, a long way down into my ankles and down into my feet. I am feeling supported as I deeply connect to Mother Earth. I allow the support of Mother Earth to ground me out of my mind and into my body.

"Imagine a light running from the crown of your head all the way down your physical body, down into the core of the Earth. Let go of all your worldly worries, let go of all that no longer serves you. Open your heart. Let go, breathe and promise never to close your beautiful heart again.

I promise to keep my heart open.

Every breath you breathe, spirals you into golden light. Golden light welcomes you to dive deep into your oceanic mind and deep into your remembering. You are journeying down into the deep sea of your superconscious mind. Say this now,

Superconscious mind, I know you're powerful and I know you're listening. I know that you will reveal three karmic beliefs to me now.

"Diving down, deeper and deeper, you enter the vast space of your akashic records. A big soup of experiences, lessons and energy swirls around you. Tell me what you see."

"I see three pink scallop shells floating towards me through the soup. The first one says I am powerless, and I can't control my emotions."

"Okay, pick it up and crush it."

I did as Mr. Sub-con said, and I instantly felt relieved.

"I did it!"

"Well done. What does the second one say?"

"It's not safe to express my needs and I don't have a voice."

"You know what to do, get rid of it."

I crushed it into dust.

"Okay, it's gone!"

"What does the last one say?"

"I am unworthy of love."

"Smash that negative belief! Crush it into nothingness and destroy it."

I obliterated the words on the shell in a surge of rage.

"Good! Now wipe the slate clean. Invoke Saint Germain's violet flame to transmute all darkness into light. Call on the violet ray to clear your core beliefs now. Bring the violet flame into the crown of your head, into your third eye, down through your throat, into your heart and feel it circulating into the stomach region, into your sexual area and into the base of your spine. Feel the violet light making its way down your thighs, into your knees, your shins, your ankles and your feet. Say this,

Great Creator, I command that these programs be pulled, cancelled or resolved on all four levels within my akashic record now.

I noticed with awe that the front of my brain began to light up and I could feel the sensation of clearing. My heart began to flow, and my auric field began to illuminate. I could see a purple light shining and pulsing even though my eyes were closed.

"Imagine in your hands you are holding three new scallop shells. I want you to write the words of your empowering beliefs on them with this golden pen. Inside this pen flows pure gold. Pure gold holds the power to heal. Say your beliefs out loud,

I am always powerfully connected to my true self and I command my subconscious to focus on the purity of love. All my thoughts and feelings are in a state of perfection. I acknowledge the divine flame within me, and I am grateful to my creator for the eternal connection that flows through me.

"Listen to your beliefs as they reverberate throughout your heart, mind, body and spirit. Write them on the shells now and, as you do, I want you to feel your empowering beliefs making their way into your information system, creating new cellular memories within you as your new programs are anchored.

"As you are writing the words, imagine sparkles of light vibrating into every part of you, every muscle, every bone, every tissue and every organ. See your akashic record clearing your old patterns of energy now. Say this now,

I am the creator of possibility, I am a magnet for all good things, I am alive with vitality and life force. I feel shimmers and light in every cell of my being. In every system, immune, endocrine, lymphatic, respiratory, excretory and reproductive system. I feel vital and alive.

"Feel a surge of power through your body now igniting courage and inspiration to be all that you are born to be. Say, yes, I am a miracle unfolding and I know I am powerful."

I am a miracle unfolding and I know I am powerful.

"Nod your head that you know this. Ruby Rose, inside you is a dream that you are longing to follow. This dream will bring purpose to your life. I want you to visualise it now."

I opened my mind and invited my dream vision to present itself, but nothing happened. I wasn't sure what to do.

"I can't see anything; I feel blocked by something."

"What are you feeling?"

"I feel sad."

"I know how to unlock it. We need to find the repressed memory that's blocking you from allowing yourself to dream. I'm going to count to three and, when I do, you will travel through time and space to the exact memory when you gave up on your dreams."

Chapter 13

DISCOVERING DREAMS

"1,2,3. You arrive on the oval and young Ruby Rose is just finishing her race. She's in year 10 and finished second. You walk up to her and give her a big hug. You shout 'Congratulations' and hand her a big bunch of flowers. She smiles, surprised to see you. Her heart immediately lifts with your support. She can instinctively feel that you love and care about her.

"You say to her, I am the older you and I've come to support you. You're an amazing runner. I'm so proud of you. Have you ever stopped to look at your achievements in athletics over the past years? Do you remember when you became the fastest runner in Tasmania for the 1500m?"

"Yes! I was in grade six."

"Do you remember that at the start of that year you had a major setback?"

"Yes, I had to recover for two months after going to hospital because my left hamstring was cut open."

"You had an accident when you were swinging on a vine in the bush and it broke."

"They had to stitch up the back of my leg."

"But you made an incredible comeback after going to hospital and, even though you had stitches across the length of your left thigh, you didn't give up. You have a natural ability to run. You're such an amazing athlete."

"Oh, no. She's starting to cry, Sub-con. What do I do?"

"Comfort and listen to her. This will be very healing because, without you, she will bottle everything up and pretend she's is okay. Take her away somewhere private so she can open up to you."

"We're sitting down at a table now. She's wiped away her tears and is looking at me."

"You've come back to congratulate me for coming second?" Ruby Rose said.

"Yes, I love you so much and there's something you need to know. I came here today to see you cross the finish line and to congratulate you for coming second because, in my eyes, you're already a winner."

Ruby Rose's face flushed with embarrassment. It was obvious she was still coming to terms with finishing second.

"How are you feeling about your race?"

"To be honest, I feel like I'm a failure," she said. "I've decided to give up on running."

"You've decided to give up on running because you came second? Most people would be happy with an achievement like that. This is your moment to step up. You have a very important choice to make. What you choose today is going to shape the rest of your life. How you view your race will determine your future opportunities for success."

"How come?"

"Well, if you give up because you didn't succeed, you will keep doing this for the rest of your life. Your fear of failure will sabotage your success. I want you to think about looking at coming second from another angle. What else could you make it mean?"

"I could make it mean that I have to train harder if I want to win and that I can't give up on myself and my talents."

"How does that make you feel?"

"It actually makes me feel more grateful and determined to follow my dreams. I could make a come-back! Instead of giving up, I could focus and set myself new goals."

"Exactly! You still have the inter-school cross-country coming up. Why don't you train for that?"

Chapter 13: Discovering Dreams

"Yes, but I ..."

"Have you been distracted lately?"

"Yes, I haven't been training."

"Don't give up on your dreams, Ruby Rose! When people ask you how you went in the school cross-country today, what are you going to say?"

"The girl who won trained very hard. She deserves it more than me, because she worked for it. I'm not going to give up, I'm going to train and keep my eyes on my goals. I know I could have won, but I haven't been prioritising the things that are actually important to me."

"I'd like you to repeat the following affirmations."

I am going to set myself goals and meet them with ease because I know my true worth. I know that I am an extraordinary human being. If I master and express the gifts that I have been given, my true potential can be fulfilled. If I ignite my dreams and lead the life of my highest potential, I will know fulfilment.

I demand my subconscious mind to imprint these core beliefs deep into my thoughts and feelings. I am good enough; I am a success and I believe in myself.

I accept that in all challenges there are hidden blessings and I focus on looking for the wins in every situation. I take notice of all the good things that are happening in my life and I let go of the rest.

I know that where my focus goes my energy flows, so I focus my thoughts on being aware of my heart. I relax deeply and begin to fill with the deep understanding that I am enough, I am extraordinary, and I am strong. Love is entering my heart and spreading its golden glow throughout my entire body.

Light is reaching into every dark crevice that has held me hostage with self-limiting beliefs, blocks and fears. I am the creator and the source of my highest potential. I choose to create powerful mantra within me – mantra that will see me step into my greatness. Sub-con paused before suggesting,

"Now older Ruby Rose, take the younger Ruby Rose in your arms. You are going to integrate the part of you that is holding fear around failing. Speak into her ear about how proud of her you are and what a success she is. Remind her to never give up.

"After you've done that, watch your younger self disappear into you. Feel her happiness in your heart that she knows the truth. I'm going to count to three and you're going to open your eyes and smile, because sparkles of truth are igniting in your life. Lock this into your mind.

I am worthy of a rich, wonderful, glorious and abundant life. I matter and I am enough. I choose to live my life mindfully. I am consciously creating every aspect of my life in every chapter – my thoughts, feelings and my mantra. I am the watchful eyes of Buddha awareness, observing my mind from the seat of my heart.

I allow life to bring people to me. The people I meet will guide me with information, knowledge and wisdom. As I journey into my greatness, I trust and surrender that I am evolving within this process. I notice it, I speak of it and I am grateful for it. I express gratitude for everything that comes into my life – every challenge and every blessing.

I am opening and expanding beyond old beliefs and old patterns. I am embracing a new way of being now. All my cells are activating on a cellular level; all my mitochondria are functioning optimally.

All electrical pulses, pathways, nerve endings, tissues and fibres are switching on. Everything is in alignment. All intelligence within me is awakening to every aspect of my mind, body, heart and spirit.

I am being brought into a self-realised state of consciousness. I give myself complete permission to be in my true self. I am witnessing and observing my mind and my emotions. I step into a deep state of awareness within me.

"Your meditation will be complete by the time I count to three.

"One, take a deep breath in and feel the vibration of your cells cleansing, revitalising and purifying all the centres in your body from the base chakra to the sacral chakra, up into the solar plexus, moving towards the heart, connecting with the throat, opening the third eye and illuminating the crown chakra.

"Two, take a nourishing breath of oxygen and feel unconditional love flooding through your body. Sigh as the feeling brings you ease and peace.

"Three, open your eyes, your heart and smile. You have now completed your upgrade and have effectively programmed yourself with empowering core beliefs. You are running systems of thought that are building new mantra within you. This is giving you the knowing, that you are worthy, you are enough, and you have a very important purpose to fulfil. Say this now,

I trust myself to take a leap of faith now. I don't need to know all the answers, but I do need to know my ultimate vision. In order to get my desired result, I need to be open to believing. I need to notice the synchronicities that are occurring around me that are assisting me to pursue my highest potential.

"What is at the core of your true potential? What is your ultimate vision?"

"I thought it was to meet my true love but now I want to love myself."

"So, your ultimate vision is self-love?"

"Yes, I'd love to transcend all limiting beliefs and live in a constant state of love within myself."

"What a beautiful vision, and so it is said, so it shall be done. Open your arms and welcome your dream into your life. Shower it with love and honour your vision. Take notice of the inspiration that is arriving."

"How do you feel when you see yourself achieving this state of being?"

"I'm feeling fantastic!"

"Become laser-focused on the details. Where are you? What are you doing? Who are you being in the community?"

"I'm teaching people to connect to their spirituality."

"When is it occurring? Why and how is it happening?"

"It's happening in the future. I'm a yogi and there is light all around me."

"See the outcome in your heart now and feel the immense pleasure your dream gives you. Feel joy rise up your spine, placing you in a golden glow of pure ecstasy. See shivers of sparkling gold bubbling through every cell in your body, as your dream builds momentum on a cellular level.

"Watch your cells applaud and cheer with happiness as you send your being into a frenzy of pure light because you are seeing the outcome of your dream existing as a reality.

"Feel the steady pulse of your heartbeat quickening with excitement as the rhythm of your dream begins to synchronise with your body and enter your existence. Say these words now:

I am in divine connection to loving myself. I am as carefree as the breeze that blows my hair. I listen to the whispers of purity and perfection within me. I am consciously choosing to connect to loving myself every day.

I commit to spending 10 minutes daily to seeing, feeling and experiencing love within myself. I enjoy doing this because I am always filled with the miracle of inspiration.

The violet flame enters my mind, heart, body and spirit when I make this connection, so it is an effortless and rewarding experience that I look forward to everyday.

I spend this time putting my energy and positive thoughts into seeing and feeling my desired results. I pray for divine assistance as I connect more and more with loving myself every day. Every day I affirm these things.

I am open to receiving a constant connection with loving myself. I am holding this vision within my heart now.

It is with complete trust that I action daily steps towards being in divine connection with my truth. My heart truly desires this dream, and I am in complete trust and faith, as I follow the light within me.

I am trusting life always. I believe in all possibilities, even those that I am yet to see. I am filled with belief that all issues are resolving and being looked after for me.

The more I focus on positive outcomes, the happier my thoughts are and the quicker my outcomes are drawn to me. As I build excitement and joy around my vision, I know that this is the first step in reaching my dream.

"Set an intention to step forward into a state of bliss and to connect with loving yourself. Visualise receiving purple light, white light and golden light. With heartfelt emotion, repeat the following statement:

I am a master at managing my state. My life is filled with inspiration and joy. I am always conscious of loving myself. I experience uplifting bliss.

"As you say it again, leap forward with an awesome fist pump, step up into a warrior pose. Stand tall and straight as you feel the light tickling your toes. Watch it move all the way to the top of your head.

"Ask your mind, body, heart and spirit to be brought into an enlightened state now. See yourself flicking a switch in your mind that says, "Self-love." Activate and focus on your heart and ask to be open to receiving a direct link to your true self. Let your heart know that it's safe for you to be connected in this way and that it's safe for you to show the world you love yourself.

"Inside every single cell and organ in your body you are seeing you dream coming true. Your energy is amplifying because the violet flame is carrying energy that transmutes all darkness into light. You are now sending a powerful force of energy throughout your entire being as you connect with your dream. Say this now:

I give my heart, body, mind and spirit the opportunity to receive my vision today.

"You are consciously nurturing a fertile ground for the seed of your vision to grow. All you need to do is seal your intention with a creation ceremony. I'd like to do this with you now."

"Sure."

Chapter 14

CREATION CEREMONY

"The reason for holding a creation ceremony is to bring your dream into your physical reality," Mr. Sub-con said. "Sit down and get comfortable. Take some time to focus on your dream. It's already in a meta-physical process and is currently synthesising into the perfect outcome for your highest good.

"We are going to seal it into physical form for you. To do this, we need ginger. I'll explain the properties of ginger later but, more importantly, the reason we're holding a creation ceremony is to offer a significant spark of life-force energy into your vision. With enough focus, commitment and practice, your dream will become your reality. Say this now:

I am open to my ultimate vision and I am ready and willing to receive it now. I am taking full responsibility for the choices I make that block my progress.

If I make a choice that is out of alignment with my dream, it is no longer acceptable for me to drop into victim mentality and start blaming others as being the reason why I'm not focusing on my dream of self-love.

Instead, the voice of empowerment will recognise my actions instantly and I will step back into my power and take responsibility for my actions. I am empowered to create lasting success in my life now.

"Repeat this declaration of commitment to your dream."

I, Ruby Rose Taylor, 1111, am empowered to take responsibility for my life circumstances. I am filling my mind with a warrior-like mentality in the pursuit of my dream.

I am taking control of all my choices surrounding my pathway to realising my journey to self-love. I am on purpose and I will fulfil my dream. I am focusing my thoughts and my mind on the here and now.

I am ready to participate in the magic of life. I am opening my heart to the beauty within me. I seek the good in all things. I joyfully declare with love and light that my inspired idea and dream is a high priority in my life.

I treat myself with extreme love and kindness during this process of growth. I recognise the value of taking care of myself so that my true potential is realised. I happily declare that I will fulfil the whisperings of my heart. I will feed my dream with positive visualisations as often as I can, using the violet flame every day.

I am gentle with my vision and careful not to expose my dream to the dangers of the world before my dream has had its chance to grow.

I protect my dream from all negative thought forms including my own and others that are destructive by nature, taking me away from realising my true potential.

I promise to pursue my dream, even if it takes a different path or direction than I imagine it might. It is with faith, trust and love that I see my dream in a state of perfection. My dream deserves unconditional love and I do not place unnecessary fear and judgement upon its beautiful nature. Upon its innocence, I commit to stand by it, to nurture it, to protect it, to love it and to believe in it. I seal this commitment to my dream by drinking ginger tea and absorbing it into my body. The pure zest of ginger awakens and solidifies this commitment and I declare that I am prepared and ready to begin the path to self-love.

I now sign with the violet flame of Saint Germain in my heart as I write my signature with this golden pen.

Signed: <u>Ruby Rose Taylor</u>

"Drink the ginger tea and taste it. It is infusing a warrior-like responsibility into your physical body. Feel your personal integrity increasing and your sense of individual choice building. By using ginger, you will see yourself as the creator of your own life.

"You no longer wait for outside circumstances to change. You will choose to create your own destiny. You, as an empowered individual, are assuming full responsibility and accountability for the consequences of all actions or inactions. You are stepping up into your greatness and connecting to your true self right now.

"You are allowing yourself to experience positive growth and have said, loud and clear on a subconscious level, that you are ready and open for this connection with yourself and that you are willing to receive inspiration right now to create this in your life. You are widening your arms and readying yourself for the flight ahead.

"You only need to trust that this is happening; your mind doesn't need to know all the details right now. You don't need to know how or when.

"It will come. When you trust that you will achieve your dream, you will feel better about following it. If you take a leap of faith, you will be guaranteed to achieve what you are dreaming of. The question is, how far can you jump?

"If you are given a guarantee of success, how quickly will you run towards it? Imagine you are a rising sun with the word "purpose" written in your spirit. Picture yourself waking up every day with the knowledge that you're following your deepest desire. How special and inspired do you feel, knowing that you are on your path and living a life that is in alignment with your higher purpose?"

"I feel very special."

"There is a powerful force at play when you set an intention to follow your dreams. When you say, 'I want to do this', 'I am aiming for that' or 'I'd like to be this', the pure power of intent creates momentum that allows the forces that be, to co-create with your desire.

"If you're not hardwired for success in the correct way, though, you might block your progress and never rise to the challenge in the first place. Or you may begin the project, abandon it and leave it half-finished and move on to something else.

"Be wary of your inner saboteur and its story defeating you in the game of life. It might sound like a little voice inside your head that makes you feel overwhelmed, imperfect or not good enough. Do you know the sound of this voice?"

"Yes, I do."

"Be aware of this little voice because it will destroy your dreams. It is hardwired to protect you from danger, so don't be fooled by it.

It will sabotage your happiness the first chance it gets. It doesn't know any better because it likes to be in control. Do yourself a favour and don't listen to that part of your subconscious mind. It can wreak havoc on your dreams."

"What do I do about it? What if I listen to it, and it sabotages my dreams?"

"Don't worry, this is why we have been teaching you Mind Mastery. To achieve your ultimate vision of self-love, you will need to be aware of what you are thinking and feeling in every moment. You will need to observe yourself and your thoughts in every second. If you aim for results, then it is easy to create success. If you don't aim for anything, then you will have nothing tangible to strive for and you won't maintain a steady increase in growth.

"The mind is a powerful force, but it can also be very distracting. Learn to breathe into your body. This will help you to observe the mind, rather than being at the mercy of it. Often people tell themselves things such as: 'I'll feel wonderful when I take my holidays; everything will be better.' 'When I retire, I'll finally be able to do what I want and I'll be a lot happier', 'I'll reclaim my life when the children move out; I'll feel less stress and more peace' or 'As soon as I leave my relationship things will get better'.

"The problem with this type of thinking is that it takes the power of now and projects it into the future. Herein lies the power or the weakness of the mind. The present moment is a choice. You can create your reality now and your empowered life in a single thought."

"Really?"

"Yes, because every thought gives you a feeling that leads you to a way of being. As you know yourself, the patterns of your thoughts and beliefs create individual programs that run in the background of your subconscious mind. Depending on the patterns you are running, this will show up as successes or failures in your life. To complete Mind Mastery you must be willing to investigate the inner mechanics and complex workings of your mind."

"It still sounds complicated to me."

"Accessing the doorway to your true self will require you to gain knowledge and awareness of the hidden and blocked parts within you. There is trauma to be faced yet and unpleasant feelings."

"Oh no!"

"You'll be fine. It's all about your beliefs, and you're doing well in the program. You now have the knowledge to replace old patterns, glitches, bugs and stories with more empowered thinking. The good news is that if you want to get rid of your blocks, you can! As a result of meeting and being with yourself in this way, you can transition into new states of awareness that make you unstoppable. It takes patience and practice to understand the 'how' and 'why' of this process but you are the only one standing in your way."

"What do you mean, I'm the only one standing in my way?"

"As human beings, we'd much rather hold on to the belief that it is our vicious ex-lover that is the problem. Or it is our business partner that's to blame. We would rather think that he or she is the real reason why we're having problems. Watch your stories and be wary because you're making an excuse.

"You might not be ready to accept it yet but, in time, you will understand. And, once you do, you will experience your life beyond the door of your old program. Be mindful, though, because there are a million and one excuses that your mind wants to trick you with. I am forewarning you now, because you don't want to get up front and personal with the doorway to your dreams and then decide, 'Oh no, I'm too busy and I have so many other things to get done' or 'What's the point anyway? I never finish anything I start'.

"Watch your stories and be aware of your thoughts, especially the ones that stop you right before you step through the door. Most of your life you have been unaware of your self-limiting beliefs but not anymore. Be clear on what level of Mind Mastery you want to achieve and visualise what it looks like in your life. Follow your visions and dreams and take the good with the bad. Whatever comes your way, know that you have the ability to create a negative situation into a positive one. Trust the wisdom in your heart to hear your inner guidance and say this now:

I am always focused on moving in the direction of my life purpose. I am listening beyond my mind. As I act, momentum builds around my dream.

As I am filled with inspiration from within, I leverage this consciously by visualising positive results. I see my success as if it is already happening in the here and now.

"I'd like to do a quick survey on your Mind Mastery. I will ask you a question and you can respond with the following responses: never, some, mostly, considerably and always. You can rate them on this scale as 1-5.

1 never
2 some
3 mostly
4 considerably
5 always

"Are you ready for the questions?"
"Yes."
"I am aware of my thoughts."
"3. Mostly."
I know my patterns from the past."
"2. Some."
"I know all my limiting core beliefs."
"2. Some."
"I know the stories I created when I formed my core beliefs."
"2. I know some of them."
"I know how to reprogram my subconscious mind."
"2. Some.
"I experience a blissful state of mind."
"2. Sometimes."
"I can change my state of mind by choice."
"4. It is considerably better now."
"I can visualise positive outcomes."
"2. Sometimes."
"I create my life consciously."
"Well ... I've only just started doing that. So sometimes."

"I choose the direction of my life."

"I'm going to say 5! Always."

"I am a master of my mind."

"Sometimes I'm a master of my mind!"

"What level of Mind Mastery do you want to achieve?"

"I'm not sure. Whatever it takes to reach my ultimate vision."

"Well, there are four levels to Mind Mastery, so it is important to set a realistic goal for yourself and to get clear about what you want to achieve. For example:

"Mind Mastery level 1: Gives you some knowledge and awareness of your thoughts that flow through your mind, but at this early stage you have no ability to observe and detach from your thoughts. You are at the mercy of your mind."

"Okay."

"Mind Mastery Level 2: Advances your mind towards having a sound understanding of the stories and beliefs that are running in the subconscious parts of you. At this level, you will be consciously reprogramming your limiting beliefs."

"I will definitely be working on this."

"Mind Mastery Level 3: Enables you to distinguish your 'story' from 'what happened' and will give you an opportunity to practise your ability to separate interpretation, perception and emotion from the events of your life and when you first formed your core beliefs. You will begin to become skilled at being aware of what activates and triggers you."

"I definitely want to be able to do that."

"Mind Mastery Level 4: Requires that you reach a high level of awareness within your mind and gives you the ability to see reactive thoughts and proactive thoughts. At this level, you will be consciously choosing empowering thoughts, beliefs, ideas and stories that enable you to reach your true self. You will know all the different parts of yourself and observe these parts in an entirely new way. You will demonstrate the knowledge and ability to use your mind as a tool for growth and expansion. You will co-create your reality at this level of mastery."

"Wow! I really want to co-create my reality."
"Do you remember the power of intention?"
"Yes!"

"To bring your dream into this physical reality, you will need to train yourself in Mind Mastery. To make your vision manifest into physical form, you will need to dedicate a certain amount of time and energy towards creating it. You can do this as a meditation practice because it calms your mind and keeps you focused.

"Another critical aspect of taking your dream into a reality is your mindset and your ability to develop awareness in your everyday life. As you step towards your desired outcome, your ability to maintain an observant state of mind will determine the speed of your success. Training yourself to be a witness unto yourself, is the foundation you need to lay first and foremost because you need to build a solid and supportive base. That base is you.

"To make your vision a reality, you will need to begin with the conscious intention of observing and watching your state. You need to practise getting to know your mind and how it reacts to things. What stories do you tell yourself when things become challenging?"

"I give up. I'm not lovable, I'm not good enough."

"Are you aware when it's going on?"

"Not really."

"Your goal in Mind Mastery is to connect to your realised self and, if you achieve this, you will become a channel for divine grace. There are several things that must be actioned to create a constant connection to your true self. To support you in achieving this, you will need to start playing with the idea of becoming an absolute powerhouse for mindfulness.

"Daydream about living in a constant state of awareness. Try to keep your ear tuned for the pitch, tone, phrasing and overall vibe of your self-love symphony. My question is, can you maintain awareness consciously for an entire day? Can you keep connected to self-love for a whole day? "

"I don't think so."

"Can you imagine your favourite happy song being played on a loop?"

"Yes, I can."

"Which song is it?"

"My favourite happy song is by Pharrell Williams."

"It's a bit like listening to your happy song for a whole day. Can you actively listen to it and stay with the song?"

"I don't know. I think I'll get bored and switch off."

"Sometimes our mind is like a gypsy traveller meandering down a windy road, wandering off the beaten path and making detours whenever it feels like it. Most of the time when we are pursuing our dreams, we really want to go straight. Straight for the gold medal and the pot of gold at the end of the rainbow, but a lot of the time our mind creates obstacles for us to jump over and detours we don't need.

"Do you have a playlist of songs that get your blood pumping and make you feel unstoppable?"

"Yes, I do."

"Can you take a minute now to think of one and start humming, singing, dancing and whistling it? This song will be your dream anchor as you step towards your vision. Think of what an anchor does for a boat. It keeps the boat from drifting this way or that and, depending on the current of the sea, the anchor will fix you into place.

"Consciously moor your boat into the harbour of self-love, drop your anchor, sit back in the sun and sing your favourite song. Choose one that represents ultimate freedom and liberation – a song that will inspire you to reconnect to loving yourself again and again.

"If, during the development of your ultimate vision, things deviate and you find that you've drifted away from the shore of your mesmerising blue sea, you will also require a song that represents anguish and pain – one that will allow you to release pent-up frustration, anger, guilt, sorrow or shame.

"This song will be important for you to play when you're feeling overwhelmed and disconnected from your inspiration. Play this one first and allow yourself to drop within, so that you can locate the edge of discontent and feel it deeply. Use the time to express yourself by crying, screaming, shaking and releasing all that is blocking you.

"After you have played this song and allowed yourself to be completely self-expressed, you can put your happy song on and return to your ultimate vision by calling it in again. Choose your two songs now and keep them on hand for the duration of actioning your dream into a reality.

"Always set an intention for what you are letting go of and what you are calling in. Any time you get knocked down, use the anguish song to get psyched back up again and, when you play your uplifting song, I want you to dance like crazy, sing your heart out and imagine all your hopes and dreams coming true.

"That sounds like a good idea."

"I'm pleased to say Ruby Rose that you have completed this part of the program successfully. You now understand the power of connecting to your subconscious mind and the process of traversing between the different states, by slowing your brainwaves. You can access your Theta brainwave and program yourself for success. You can do this by commanding me, your subconscious mind directly.

"You can also guide yourself into a deep state of meditation and heal limiting thoughts, feelings and beliefs. You can monitor your own thoughts and beliefs to ensure you are empowered for self-love. If, at any stage something comes up that blocks you, all you must do is say to your conscious mind,

I am ready to tap into my subconscious mind and allow whatever memory or belief to surface that is standing in the way of my true self.

"You can go back into any memory and simply alter the event before it happened and turn it into a powerful win. I am always with you, Ruby Rose. You can command me at any moment to do anything you want. That is how powerful you really are."

"Thank you. Sub-con. I really appreciate learning so much from you."

"You're welcome. Keep up the great work. I'm taking you back to the glade now, where you first started. I'd like you to dial up to another universal provider. Put in your pin code and access Heart Consciousness. The next phase of the program is called Happy Heart."

"That sounds nice. Thank you Sub-con."

"You're welcome."

Chapter 15

HAPPY HEART

Staring into the deep reflections on the surface of the beautiful lake in Monet's glade, I pondered my Mind Mastery techniques. The flying horse named Pegasus with its magical wings was nowhere to be seen but the rabbits were still nibbling quietly on the grass. In my mind, I said, I am Ruby Rose Taylor, 1111, and I am ready to connect to Heart Consciousness now. All love and all light now to me, all love and all light now to me."

"Ruby Rose, I want you to know how loved you are."

"Jesus!" I was staring at the handsome prince of peace himself.

"I am Jeshua, please refer to me as your brother. Many religions have misinterpreted my teachings and my name may stop people from opening their hearts."

"Ok Jeshua." My brother placed his left hand over his heart and then his right. He closed his eyes and took a deep breath in. He nodded at me to do the same.

"Can you feel a soft, gentle touch of warmth spreading into your chest?"

"Yes."

"Can you say, I love you, Ruby Rose?"

"Sure. I love you, Ruby Rose."

"Can you say, I honour your love, I cherish your love and I see your love?"

"Yes, I honour your love, I cherish your love and I see your love."

"This is a gift you can give to yourself at any time. Your gift of love. There's something I want you to know, dear one."

"What is it?"

"You are loved more than you can possibly imagine."

"I am?"

"Yes. The universal source of all that is, loves every part of you."

"It does?"

"Yes."

"Do you think you can try to feel this love?"

"I don't know."

"If you can hold the vibration of love for more than 20 seconds, you will begin to feel it. Place your hands on your heart, bow your head to your heart and let your mind know that it is in service to your heart. Your heart and higher self, hold the highest power."

I bowed my head to my heart, and I released fear. I breathed in safety and security.

"Close your eyes and direct love into your heart."

I focused on my heart for 20 seconds. A feeling of peace began to grow, and I noticed love moving through me. A flood of warmth moved inside my chest.

"Just imagine that your heart is responding to your love and is transforming your heart with glitter and sparkles. Can you see it?"

"Yes, I can! Wow, it is so beautiful! My heart is twirling and spinning. It's suspended in time and space. It's so magical."

"Wonderful! Now imagine that your love is connected to the universal heart of all that is. Visualise your heart opening to the divine mother of all hearts."

"My heart is vibrating, and I can feel it opening."

"Great! Can you see that within your heart there is a deeper level available to you now?"

"Yes."

"Within the core of your heart there is a chamber waiting to be opened."

"A chamber?"

"Yes. I want you to watch as an opening reveals a very deep part of you."

"Wow! I'm opening the door now."

"Peer into the depth of your heart, feel into this space within you and witness who you truly are."

"I am a being of love and light!"

"When you are ready, I want you to feel the love I'm sending you. Are you open, willing and ready to receive it?"

"I am."

"I'm sending it now."

I instantly felt a flood of peace filling every cell in my body and my heart began to open like a flower. I sighed with relief as I received healing light.

"Expand this feeling, so that it fills every part of you with the resounding sensation of peace."

"Oh, it's so beautiful. I'm really feeling it."

"Wow! Did you see that?" Jeshua said.

"A white dove called the Spirit of Love flew out of your heart! It's spreading white light all around you."

"Oh, my goodness! It's so beautiful. It's showering me with self-love and bringing me the gift of inner peace. White light is moving through my body and entering my cells. The dove is letting me know that it is safe for me to receive love."

"Yes, it is safe for you to receive love; from yourself, from me, from others and from the universal heart, too. Let go of anything that's been stuck inside you and trust that it's okay to soften into love now."

I sighed and opened my palms to receive love.

"Can you see the colour green pouring into your heart now?"

"Yes, I can."

"Did you notice, as soon as you moved your palms into an open position, you became more receptive?"

"Yeah!"

"Your heart naturally wants to connect to love, so release anything that feels fearful within you. Connect into your heart and feel what needs to be released. I'm sensing that you are afraid of getting hurt?"

"Yes, I am."

"Are you fearful of men because of this?"
"Yes."
"Are you scared to trust men?"
"Yes."
"Can you meet this fear within you?"
"I don't know."
"Allow your heart to surrender and let go of any darkness suffocating your ability to meet your deepest shadows. Let go and breathe."
"I'll try."
"Go to the edge of fear within you and feel the depth of your fear around trusting men."

I began to sob.

"I'm not sure I can do it. There's too much pain."
"We all need healing and you've come to Earth to learn. Everything serves and that's why it's important to learn your lessons and let go. We've all got shadows, and no-one is perfect. If you can learn to love yourself while seeing your own shadows and send love to your shadows, you will learn to love others for their shadows, too. As you become familiar with the different parts of your personality, you can bring more awareness to your triggers."
"My triggers?"
"Yes."
"What are they?"
"The things that make you reactive."
"Oh."
"What happens when something triggers you, is that everything you are reacting to is actually coming from your subconscious mind."
"Oh yeah, Sub-con was teaching me that."
"Remember, how you learnt that the subconscious mind remembers everything and that your entire life is stored in the background?"
"Yes."

"Well, nine times out of 10, you can guarantee that when you experience a reaction towards something, it's actually your past that is triggering your fight, flight or freeze response. Once you have been triggered, getting to the root cause is essential. A story, memory or a belief system is causing you to react. This the real reason you are triggering.

"Once you've been triggered, though, it can be very difficult to isolate the underlying issue, because you're usually processing intense emotions and feelings inside the body. Usually, there is a coupled-up effect going on."

"A coupled-up effect?"

"Yeah, usually after the event has calmed down, you can take yourself through some personal inquiry. By doing this, you will discover the source of your trauma. It is usually deeper than the present issue at hand. The tricky part of post-traumatic stress is that it can be years after an event has occurred that the damage to your psyche is revealed. Let me show you something you will never forget. I'm so glad you made it through the Mind Mastery program because your life is just getting started. Are you ready to connect, to see the true wonder of your worth?"

"Yes, I'd love to see the true wonder of my worth."

"I can see that you truly are! Your eyes are sparkling with inner light and specks of gold are lighting up your face. You have found your way and journeyed to the path of your divine light and you're about to practise self-love. This is the secret to finding true love."

"Really?"

"Yes. When we make space for ourselves, to know ourselves, to feel ourselves, to love ourselves and to connect to ourselves, then we can share our love. Often, we are running on empty, and we don't even know it. We can't find the love within us. But when we have the love within us, we can come from a place that is full and overflowing. Without self-love, you feel afflicted, stressed, worried and consumed. This is not a place to be able to give love from.

"When you set aside time for a practice that is absolutely dedicated to self-love and nurturing yourself, then you can truly heal yourself. You are a creator, but you are also a destroyer. You can see light, but you can also see dark. You can choose what is good or bad and you can stay, or you can go. You are free. It is you who decides your destiny."

"Yes, I can see how I choose my destiny."

"You are going to journey deeper now. Deep into your heart, for it is on this journey that you will become reborn. As you journey, you're going to lose all sense of time. Time is an illusion, so allow yourself to stay present and in the moment. Use your breath and your senses to keep you in the here and now. That way your connection to your truth will remain.

"If your mind starts to wander, simply exhale and let go; if you begin to lose connection with your body, just pause and remember that golden light is flowing to you from above your crown and making its way down your spine, grounding you deeply, so deeply that any feelings of insecurity around loving yourself begin to make way for a renewed sense of earthly belonging. Are you ready?"

"Yes."

Chapter 16

ROSES OF LOVE

Jeshua started me on my journey to rebirth.
"If you love who you are, accept who you are and stand for who you are. As a human being, you are sending a strong and empowered message to yourself and others:
This is me. I love who I am, and I am happy with who I am.
"To realise self-love, you need to work on your self-love muscles. If you practise a daily workout of honouring, appreciating and being with yourself in a positive way, and nurturing a space of self-acceptance within you, then you will naturally love who you are because who you are is especially nourishing, supportive and kind."

"It sounds really lovely."

"It is. See the world through rose-coloured glasses for a moment and visualise a loving image of yourself, filled with happiness and light. Above you is a hot-air balloon with a large basket coming down from the heavens. Can you see it?"

"Yes, it's hovering towards me now."

"Put all your unloving thoughts into it."

"Okay."

"You are getting rid of anything that is holding you back from feeling self-love."

"Okay."

"Release any depressing conversations that you've been having with yourself. Let go of anything that has been shrouding you in pain, so you can finally be free."

"Okay."

"You are now releasing the energy that has been toxic to your mind, body, heart and spirit. Send it into the basket and when you've unloaded all your negative energy, let me know."

I spent a long time thinking about all the things that happened with Sam and the stress of going through the abortion. I thought about all my limiting beliefs and then sent away my obsessive negativity that had begun to take over my mind. When I felt ready, I nodded assent.

"Now, watch as the balloon begins to take off with all your baggage and drama. Let the demons you've been carrying be lifted high into the sky. Watch as the weight of darkness begins to leave you now."

"Can you see two angels at the top of the balloon waving to you?"

"I can."

"They're smiling at you in their loving, caring way. Now they are guiding the basket far, far away into another realm. They're taking it into the light for you."

"Really?"

"Yes, they're taking it to a place where divine love is so bright that negative emotions, memories and feelings instantly dissolve."

"Amazing!"

An angel taps me on the head with her wand and says, "You're so special!"

"I am so special!" I grin from ear to ear with happiness and love for myself.

"The angels are dropping all your limiting thoughts and beliefs into a black hole. All your unnecessary data is being poured into a swirling abyss, mingling with the beauty of the cosmos itself. The dark matter that has been taking up space in your heart is disappearing as if magic as it is cleansed with photons, neutrons and electrons. All your dense particles are being transformed into the violet flame of Saint Germain and you are becoming an iridescent star of truth as spirit cancels, clears and resolves all that no longer serves your beautiful heart."

I started to cry; I was feeling so loved.

"Thank you!"

"Take a deep breath in, the deepest breath you've taken for a very long time."

I began to feel relieved. For the first time in eons, something deep within me was being released.

"Spirit is pouring love into your entire system. Can you feel the lightness in your being now?"

"Yes, I can."

"As you breathe light into your inner galaxy of oxygen, hydrogen and nitrogen, you breathe out carbon dioxide. Watch the rise and fall of your expansion and contraction. Just as the universe pulses and breathes, so do you. Focus your attention on creating peace within your heart. Feel calm and serene. Open your heart with softness and accept all that is.

"Can you feel your heart expanding a fraction more as you practise receiving self-love?"

"It's a bit difficult."

"Don't worry if a 'Do Not Enter' sign is stuck around your heart right now. With time and patience, you will heal your heart into happiness again. Hold your hands to your heart and say this now:

I am enough, I am happy, I am whole, and I am complete.

"Say it three times, special one. I know it's a simple statement, but when you attach emotion to these words you begin to fill with a sense of ease and bliss.

I am enough, I am happy, I am whole, and I am complete.

I am enough, I am happy, I am whole, and I am complete.

"Imagine now that your happiness is growing brighter by the second and you are entering a special place within you – a special place, filled with joy and laughter. A space where you feel completely at home. You feel connected, safe and secure. You're not struggling or feeling limited in this place.

"Imagine this space within you is like a doorway to your very own secret garden of self-love. As you twist the knob, your doorway to the light swings wide open. You peek inside and notice the beauty of the light that is filtering through and illuminating the flowers and roses growing there. The light looks like floating fragments of magic. It's spectacular and looks amazing, but what are you feeling?"

I feel weightless,
I'm as light as a feather,
I am floating inside light itself,
Dissolving as one and becoming it.
I am completely suspended within its beauty,
I can feel it spreading throughout my body,
There is nothing in my mind, not a single thought.
Just complete silence and peace,
It's so beautiful,
The light is spreading down my toes,
Up my fingers and I'm feeling so much love within me.

"Take a long, nourishing breath and focus your attention on your nostrils. Fill your nose with the sweet scent of nature's vital life force. Feel the oxygen cleansing your cells with clean air as you inhale and exhale. Feel your feet sinking deeply into the Earth.

"Touch the soft grass and relax your body as you sit cross-legged. Take another slow, deep breath in and place one hand below your navel and the other above your belly button. Feel the warmth from your hands spread all around your stomach and, from this place of support, imagine a golden sun emanating from the back of your spine. Chant the word 'Aum' and listen to the sound as it vibrates inwardly and outwardly, running up and down your spine, expanding your energy field.

"As you concentrate on your breath, fix your gaze on the bright red roses growing wild and free in this golden garden of love. One of the roses captures your attention. You get up and move closer. It is delicate and strong. You admire its form and shape. Observing the structure of its elegant existence, you rest your eyes on its soft petals. You lean your face into its bounty and take a deep, invigorating inhalation of its sweet scent. You can smell beauty, kindness and compassion spreading into your heart. You say to yourself;

I command my subconscious mind to believe that I am lovable. I allow my heart to feel it, my body to embrace it and my soul to connect to it. I command my subconscious mind to accept that I am enough, and I allow my heart to feel the deep, deep resonance of being enough.

I give my body permission to breathe with sweet relief as this belief enters my being. I am enough. My soul dances; knowing my truth. Subconscious mind, I command you to let go of all self-hatred and all inner criticism now. I ask you to connect to my truth and my divinity.

I fill the biology of my body with the belief that I am lovable. I am incredible and I am a magical being of light. I am a magnificent being, born of compassion, courage and confidence. This wisdom of inner peace spreads into every cell in my body, into every aspect of who I am; right down to my very soul. I am always connected to the divine light that sends me an endless stream of love."

I am lovable, I really am. I deserve to feel good about who I am. The light from Father Sky connects me to my inner sun. My solar plexus shines. I feel peace knowing and remembering my inner jewels of beauty. I am cells of love and light. I am perfect, just as I am.

Looking up from the roses in the garden; you see the yellow sun in the sky. You watch as the Creator spreads the heavens for you. The words, 'I am lovable' dance in the air. You laugh with childlike playfulness because your reality is changing, and you are seeing the world through new eyes.

Taking a paintbrush and a palette of colours, you become the creator of your experience. You paint a forest at the end of the glade and put magical sparkles in the sky. You set the sun with a magnificent display of colours and you watch for a while as the colours in the landscape blend together. You rise the moon and make a little wish as you paint an illuminated pathway through the glade. You're having fun, and butterflies are dancing as the magic of your creativity shimmers with the moonlight Oh, what a glorious night for your self-love healing! Follow your own path in this life, Ruby Rose. Trust your intuition as you come to an opening in the garden where roses bloom with their own beauty everywhere! Here you will be bathed in the glorious medicine of self-love, self-acceptance and self-forgiveness.

Dew drops are sparkling like diamonds upon you as the moon's silver light showers into your heart. Keep following your path, Ruby Rose, all the way to the edge of the glade. The voice of Jeshua was guiding me.

"Slow down when you notice a slight breeze moving through the trees. Dapples of light are casting shadows throughout the forest here. Notice the light and the dark; simply observe its existence in nature."

A warm glow enters your heart, readying you for surrender. You instinctively know what to do and say. You command your subconscious mind to surrender and let go.

Subconscious mind, I command you to surrender and to let go. I allow my heart to feel the light and the dark within me. I choose to release and renew my heart now.

Inside the darkness of the forest you see a wooden cabin. This is a sacred healing place. Your conscious mind slows and stops. Your subconscious mind relaxes and breathes. You begin to intuitively release past patterns associated with low self-esteem. It's as though you remember who you really are and why you have come to this special place. A sudden surge of inspiration awakens your spirit, and you choose to change your life. You choose to love yourself. Words of affirmation and truth speak through you.

I allow peace and tranquillity to enter my body, heart, mind and spirit. I am creating an oasis of peace, love and happiness within me now. I am ready to re-create and restore my energy to vitality. I am ready to love myself.

In the safety and protection of the forest, you step towards the log cabin. With each step, painful thoughts and beliefs begin to rise to the surface. As you take a breath of sweet, clean air, all the plants send you love and peace.

"It's okay to face your demons now and love yourself," they gently whisper. "You are worth it, and you are beautiful."

The plants melt your insecurity, easing all the tension in your body and allowing you to let it all out. All the pain of your past relationships, the betrayal, control and emotional manipulation and finally the trauma of your abortion begins to release."

Tears stream down my face and deep-seated feelings of pain crack open. I could feel the depth of my emotions coming to the surface. The plants were swaying gently. Moving forwards and backwards as they continued to send me their love and reassure me that it was safe to let go and heal now.

Breathing in deeply, I let it all go. With every breath in and every breath out, the pain melted from my mind, body, heart and spirit. The memories, thoughts and feelings towards myself and the men I'd been involved with began to burn away.

Chapter 17

CHANGING TIDES

I made my way slowly to the porch steps; I could feel the gentle creaking of the wood beneath my feet and as I turned the knob on the door; it felt soft and welcoming. I entered a room lit by candles and, as my eyes adjusted to the dim light, I could smell an aroma of pleasant vanilla spice blending with the cedar walls of the cabin. Jeshua guided me.

"Bring your awareness to the presence of Mother Earth and imagine that she is holding you and loving you in this moment. Take some deep breaths as you feel the Earth connecting, stabilising, grounding and holding you. Command your subconscious mind now,

Subconscious mind open the bottom of my spine with the colour red and release any negative thought forms, parasitic entities, or programs on all four levels of my existence. Remove limiting core beliefs from this life, from all my ancestors carrying traumatic genetic memory. Release all trauma now.

Clear stagnant energy and disturbed memories that are within the base chakra that may be inhibiting my path to self-love. Any collective consciousness blocking self-love, please remove it now. Anything on a soul level that is contained within my base chakra, I ask it to be pulled and replaced with a deep sense of security, belonging, worthiness and love.

"As you drop deeper and deeper into the base chakra, into your old stories, your old patterning and all your old programs, command the presence of the Great Creator of all that is.

Great Creator, I command that you assist with this healing.

"Drop deeper into the base chakra, deep into Mother Earth's grounding heart and her spirit. Command white light to come through your crown. Blue light through your third eye. And the violet flame through the auric field to stabilise and harmonise your entire system.

"Release all your demons, all your negative entities, all curses, all oaths and vows from past lives and from this life. Release anything from the feet, into the earth. Feel the weight and the chains of your past releasing now. Say this now,

White light, white light, fill my whole, dark night, dark night, I release you, and I release the demons and monsters of my past. I release you now. White light, white light, I surrender. I surrender the generations and the pain being held in my cells. White light, white light, release me. Blue ray, blue ray, hold me strong and violet flame, fire, fire. Wash away pain. Release me, release me now. I choose freedom, I choose love. Protect me now. I am love and I am loved.

"Command the Great Creator to give you an upgrade in your base chakra.

Great Creator, I command the feeling of self-love to be programmed and grounded into my base chakra. Deep in my being, deep in the soil below me and deep into Mother Earth.

"Pray for the collective. Pray that the entire planet begins to feel this ripple of self-love.

I pray in the name of Jeshua, dear God may the entire planet feel the vibration of self-love.

"Pray for the generations connected cell by cell in your lineage, may they also receive this upgrade too and that your soul, your effervescent and illuminating light is taken up into God's light and everything is purged for you in God's healing light."

I pray in the name of Jeshua. Dear God, may the generations connected to me in my cells, receive this upgrade too. May my soul be taken into God's light and all my darkness purged. May this take place as healing light enters my being. I release the energy that has held my soul from its love and from its light.

Thank you, Mother, for holding this, thank you, Creator, for taking this. Thank you, soul, for releasing this. Thank you, heart, for clearing all that is not of the light and not of my true self. Thank you, body, for expelling this, thank you, cells, for releasing this toxicity. Thank you, subconscious mind, for my new program; I am loved.

Chapter 17: Changing Tides

"Now rise and stretch out your arms to the heavens and draw a symmetrical arc downwards from the left and right as you collect anything in your auric field, any psychic dust from others, negative energy, your own thoughts and feelings, your own confusions, your own doubts and your own fears. As you draw your arms down, place your palms on the ground and say thank you, Mother Earth."

Thank you, Mother Earth, thank you, thank you, thank you.

"White light is pouring down through your crown, purifying your system – regenerating your life force; releasing and rejuvenating your being. Blue light is gliding through your third eye – awakening your inner knowing and your truth. The violet flame is clearing your auric field, clearing your mind, throat, heart, digestive system, solar plexus, and your base chakra. Sing from the base chakra,

I am loved!

"We always speak of being in love with others, but now we are speaking of being in love with ourselves. Support ourselves, rejoice in ourselves, and bring light and freedom into our being. Contract the anus, the sex organs and then let go. Contract and let go. Contract and let go. Gently pulse the energy centre with vibrant life force. As we pulse, we sing,

I'm in love, I'm in love, I'm in love.

"Imagine a glorious rich river the colour red streaming into your centre as you sing:

I'm in love, I'm in love, I'm in love. I am worthy of self-love and nourishment, I'm in love, I'm in love, I'm in love. I choose this moment to give my deepest love to my heart, my deepest soul to myself, my deepest longing to my body.

I'm in love, I'm in love, I'm in love. I call upon the powerful healer within me to be activated on all four levels to heal my wounds, afflictions, negative thoughts and negative behaviours. My all-powerful true self heals and loves me.

I am unconditionally accepting of myself, my journey, what I need and what is healing for me. I choose to honour myself first. I choose to commit to myself, to my being, to my light, my love, to my freedom, to my grace and to my eternal sunshine.

"Your healing is complete. Make your way outside to the path you created and follow your way back to the glade." I made my way to the magical path and skipped with a lightness I hadn't felt in years! Wow, what a wonderful healing! I did it, I released everything that was holding me back from seeing my truth and my beautiful essence. I am truly blessed, and I am so loved! I don't have to live stuck in my past any longer!

I can create a life for myself, exactly as I choose and think it to be. I am a powerful creator; anything I choose can be done and it is my wish to be free. I feel so deeply connected, safe and loved. I was smiling so deeply from within, that my heart felt it might burst.

"Well done, Ruby Rose. You have released all that no longer serves you and found your happy heart. It is so beautiful to witness your transformation and your willingness to heal yourself."

"Thank you, Jeshua. Thank you so much!"

"It's time for me to leave, but remember I am always in your heart. I hope you know that now. All I've ever wanted for people is to know the kingdom of love is within. The love of the divine is formed within the light of our own hearts. Please spread that message for me. The true church is the temple within."

"Yes! I certainly will! Thank you for healing my heart."

"You did the healing, I simply showed you the way. Connect to me anytime through heart consciousness."

"I definitely will brother, thank you." I stared at the beautiful spring night, feeling a deep sense of self-love within me. To my surprise, three giant-sized sunflowers walked over and were peering expectantly at me. They started laughing and singing. Four blue wrens started flying towards me and landed on my shoulder. They started tickling me. I laughed and laughed. They said, 'You're entering spring! You're entering spring! You're doing it! C'mon, let's take you on an adventure to celebrate!"

They each grabbed a corner of my clothes and up, up we flew. High into the sky we went, until Pegasus the magical white horse, came to greet us.

Chapter 17: Changing Tides

"Pegasus!" I said, recognising the breathtaking horse at once. "You're beautiful, Pegasus."

"Thank you," Pegasus said. "How are you?"

"I am loved! I am loved! I am loved!"

Pegasus gently nuzzled me and said, "Let's fly higher into the sky and, as we do, imagine all your dreams coming true. As we fly together, feel your heart lift and feel the depth of your bliss. Once you have done that, you will see a white light shining through you and soon you will forget everything but the feeling of being so incredibly high. "Here we go!"

Pegasus was right. The instant I flew into the sky, my mind began to shine like the sun. I felt alive. I was so happy and free. I was so high, I could see how small my problems looked.

Pegasus spoke in his wise voice. "Problems don't actually exist and they're not even real. They're created in the mind."

We made our way higher into the sky, flying into a rainbow. The rainbow wrapped me up in a bundle of colour, as snug as little baby, and I felt all the colours shining through me.

First the red, which smelt like strawberries, and was so delicious I really wanted to eat them!

Then orange! That part of the rainbow felt bright and warm like the sun was giving me a big hug. I could have stayed inside the beautiful golden glow for an eternity, but then yellow came and picked me up. He started shooting yellow paint out of his gun, straight at me. I was starting to get yellow! The fight was on! My inner warrior started chanting,

"You cannot defeat me, for I am strong and brave. I snatched the gun."

"Ahhhaaaa," I shot the yellow in the rainbow until, suddenly, all his yellow colour started to drain away, like he was dying. I got a bit scared.

"Oh no!" I said, "Are you okay? I think you're losing colour. Are you dying?"

The yellow part of the rainbow looked up at me and laughed,

"Got you!" His face turned from looking like he was in pain to a massive big grin that spread across his face,

"Ha-ha!" We started laughing hysterically as both of us were wrapped up in yellow together. Then green came out to play.

Green said, "Oh, I love you! You are wonderful. How's your heart?"

"How is my heart? It's fantastic!" Green pulled out a beautiful heart-shaped emerald. I stared in wonder and amazement at the beautiful jewel; I had never seen anything so beautiful.

"Look what happens when you say nice things to yourself, the gem shines brighter. Try saying something like, I am wonderful!"

"Okay! I said, eager to see what would happen,

"*I am wonderful!*" The emerald gem began to glow a beautiful green colour.

"Wow, say something else!" Green rainbow exclaimed. Getting excited, the gem started to dance.

"*I love myself and others!*" The emerald shone brighter and brighter. Reflections of light started to bounce around the room.

"*I am awesome! I am great, I am smart, I am alive, I love life.*"

"Wow!" The gem started to spin and suddenly a wizard spun from it wearing a blue and purple robe!

"Wow! Who are you?" I breathed in wonder. I hadn't expected to see a wizard today! Green was hiding behind me, a little afraid.

"Yes, who are you?" He'd never seen the wizard come from the stone either, and was shocked.

Then the wizard started to sing to me, "When you step one step and you're going straight ahead, you got the goal at the end of the rainbow, and you know you're heading there, your heart says yes and your soul is on fire. So, rise on up, step on up, let's get to it, put your mind to it, you can do it!

"Anything is possible, anything is possible, anything is possible!

"Wow!" breathed Green. "This is incredible; anything is possible!"

Pegasus flew higher and higher into the sky. "It's time to meet Lord Shiva. The final stage of the program is near."

"Really? Am I that close to finishing?
"Yes, you are."
"Who is Lord Shiva?"
"Lord Shiva is considered the Adi Yogi – the source of yoga. He discovered there are 112 ways in which a human being can attain their ultimate nature. These ways relate to the 112 chakra points in the body. You will learn to yoke the powers of your mind, body, heart and soul to commune with the supreme spirit."

"Wow, that sounds incredible."

"Lord Shiva represents the ultimate reality, the absolute and the liberator. He is one of the gods in the Hindu trinity with Brahma and Vishnu. He is the destroyer and the transformer of the universe. He is a master of supreme consciousness."

"What is that?"

"The consciousness of the soul."

"The soul has a consciousness?"

The soul is a supreme state of being."

"How?"

"It is eternal and all-knowing. Reaching supreme consciousness is attaining oneness.

"Oneness?"

"Yes."

"What's that?"

"It's remembering that we are all connected. That the eternal truth is love. Love is in you, in all creation and everywhere. The mind cannot comprehend this, so Lord Shiva will show you how to go beyond your mind so you can experience the eternal truth."

"Wow."

"Do you know the meaning of yoga?"

"No, I've practised it for many years, but I don't know what it means."

"I doubt you've been practising the traditional form of yoga because it pre-dates written history. Yoga means "union" and what you will learn today will unite human consciousness with divine consciousness."

Spiritual Spring

"I never realised yoga was about consciousness."

"That's because when yoga was brought to the Western world, its traditions got left behind. Only seekers who study the path of yoga discover the truth. As the path unfolds, you will awaken to knowing that everything is permeated by the Supreme Universal Spirit and you will experience true union with the oneness of existence. Liberation will free you from pain and sorrow.

"But now, your present state of consciousness is limited by your senses, so it takes discipline to go beyond your physical experience. Beyond this physical plane is an unfathomable consciousness on the astral plane and, even beyond this, is the infinite pure consciousness of the soul."

"Wow!"

"Can you see the sun rising through the clouds and the light shining upon the valley?"

"Yes."

"It's showing us the vastness and beauty of life. You are about to learn techniques and methods to lift the veil of illusion from your obscuring, distracting and desirous thoughts. This is the most meaningful path of life."

"Wow, it sounds amazing!"

"Can you see the sun casting its glorious rays upon you?"

"Yes, it's spectacular."

"Golden hues of pink and orange are mirroring your absolute and divine perfection. The grace of love is moving through you, offering a gift to you. Are you ready, willing and open to receive your gift of supreme consciousness?"

"Yes, I am."

Pegasus flew up to a very high mountain range and landed at the entrance of a cave.

"Good luck, Ruby Rose, I know you can do it!"

"Thank you, Pegasus!"

Chapter 18

SOARING SPIRIT

I am Ruby Rose Taylor, 1111. I am open, willing and ready to receive supreme consciousness now."

"Ruby Rose!"

"Lord Shiva?"

The majestic eyes of a wise and loving soul greeted me from the darkness of the cave. As he approached me, I noticed that his skin was covered in luminous blue paint. My eyes widened with surprise as he began sweeping a gold trident across my heart.

"I can destroy your ego with my trishul."

"What?"

"My trishul can awaken your shakti energy so that the ida, pingala and sushumna channels meet at your ajna."

"I have no idea what you're talking about? Is it going to hurt me?"

"I will only use my trishul to destroy your demons and restore your divinity!"

"That's perfect!"

Half of Lord Shiva's long brown hair was piled into a bun on the top of his head. Around his neck, a hissing green snake was coming towards me. I recoiled in fear.

"I hear you have been on quite a journey, Ruby Rose."

"Yes! It's been the most expansive journey of my life. I turned away from the snake and stepped back from Lord Shiva, focusing my gaze on the setting sun.

"I've been learning things about myself that I didn't know were possible. I've begun to see that there are many parts that make up who I am."

"What parts are they?"

"My subconscious mind, my inner child, my inner critic, my heart and my higher self."

Lord Shiva smiled with delight at my growing awareness. I couldn't help but laugh with the light of my own knowing. I spoke to the sky.

"Oh, thank you life, for bringing me here."

Lord Shiva joined me in admiring the sunset.

"Wow, the golden sun is growing brighter by the second. Let us be still. Let us sit together and begin a yogic practice in silence. As we do, I want you to observe the state of your mind. Be the sage and watch your samskaras forming like the clouds that are moving here. Simply be a witness."

"Samskaras?"

"We call samskaras your thoughts, which are actually mental disturbances or impressions that, if go unnoticed, set up impulses and trains of thought in the mind."

"Oh."

"All thoughts lead to illusion. When samskaras enter the mind, they hinder you from sighting your soul. Your mind is the king of your senses. Your organs of sensation – your eyes, ears, tongue and nose – can be mastered by breathing. Simply follow your breath and observe. Can you do that?"

"Sure."

"Now, move your breath rhythmically with a controlled, sustained sound, like this."

Lord Shiva demonstrated the technique. I did as he said and began to feel very calm.

"Focus your eyes on a fixed point and concentrate absolutely on supreme consciousness. If you want to be of service to humankind, access your spiritual power now."

"Okay."

"When we are concentrating during meditation, we are trying to shut out the experience of sense consciousness by clearing a space, so we can focus on or visualise the ishta."

"Ishta?"

"Yes, Ishta is another name for God, the Universe, Source, Spirit, Creator or Brahman. Focus on a name that feels right for you."

"I choose God."

"You also need to control your organs of action; so, no speaking, moving hands, feet, anus or genitals. By focusing on God and not getting distracted, you can leave your ego behind. If you open your heart with love for God and fix your consciousness on your creator, he will appear. The king of your mind is your soul and controlling your breath creates prana, which is vital life force energy. Building up prana and restraining mental consciousness is the key to Samadhi."

"Samadhi?"

"If you become focused internally and stop your stream of thoughts, you will experience Samadhi. It is a state of profound bliss. The mind dissolves and an absolute state of existence is reached."

"That sounds amazing."

"It is an ecstatic experience of oneness. Now focus your loving gaze with the intention of connecting to your ishta and sit in the lotus position."

Lord Shiva demonstrated the pose."

"Ow, that's really painful."

"It's only the mind that names it painful; to the body, it is just a sensation."

"I don't think I can do it."

"You can sit cross-legged. When you've become more practised, use the lotus position. Set your intention and say,

I am Ruby Rose Taylor, I am 1111. I am now connecting to my true self to realise my God-self, my divine light and my eternal love. I am concentrating on a direct connection with God force energy.

"Now concentrate on a fixed point, choose something to focus on and meditate upon God. We will be in this position for one hour."

I watched my thoughts forming like clouds. I concentrated my attention on reaching God: I smiled at him with love in my eyes, I honoured him, I prayed to him, I looked for him and, as an hour passed and my reality dissolved into God-force energy, I heard Him say,

"You are a supreme being of consciousness. You have awakened on the causal plane. There is much work to be done here."

I felt tears welling in my eyes, as my heart opened.

"Your determination and commitment to reach supreme consciousness is to be commended. As part of your spiritual growth, it is important that you realise that you are giving a great service to humanity by awakening your kundalini and harnessing your spiritual power."

"Awakening my kundalini?"

"Yes, your kundalini. It is the divine potential within you, but impressions of fear are stopping you from awakening your power."

"How does my spiritual power work?"

"It comes from the great cosmic mother, Kali. She is the one who gives birth to all. Her force awakens kundalini and her shakti energy is the life-giving, creative force that shaped your existence inside the womb. After birth, though, the material world ignited your senses and so your spiritual blueprint went into hibernation.

"Kundalini is still working quietly in the background – managing your autonomic functions, dividing your cells, assisting digestion, breathing and controlling your blood flow. If Kundalini reactivates, she will destroy your insecurities, fear, ego, ambitions, desires and separation."

"What does she look like?"

"Metaphorically speaking, she is a snake coiled in three and a half circles at the base of your spine. To awaken her, you must become desireless and content within. When Kundalini hisses like a snake, she rouses herself in mooladhara."

"Mooladhara?"

"The shakti energy centre located at the base of your spine. Her head is blocking the sushumna channel but, when she awakens, the energy moves up the central channel through the chakras. All agitations in your egoic mind disappear as she enters your heart, and the lotus of your spiritual awakening blooms."

"They didn't teach me this at the yoga studio."

"That's because most people think yoga is a fitness regime, but it's actually a scientific practice that connects you to oneness consciousness. If you are unaffected by everyone and everything, then nothing can influence you. If you can free yourself from attachment, malice, vanity and doubts, then the outside world will have no power over you. If you constantly question what's real and unreal, you will escape all illusion."

In that moment God dropped a seed into my being and I saw an image of a snake rising. My seed of supreme consciousness was being nurtured by God and my connection to the divine mother was forming.

"You can chant Om Kali Ma to connect to Kali energy."

Om Kali Ma, Om Kali Ma, Om Kali Ma.

I asked God, "So how do you create everything?"

"With love," He said. "But the purity of this love is unimaginable; you can't possibly understand it. To understand it, you can try practising non-attachment in your relationships. Treat everything as pure love and then thoughts only of now will matter.

"Expectations, attachment, "owning a person" are all fear-based and rooted in the mind. Pure love for one another is free from attachment. This is self-realisation and supreme consciousness, because we are already one."

"Thank you, God, for bringing me here."

"You heard the call. Deep within your soul, you cried out for this. I am merely answering your spiritual call for guidance, love and healing. The spiritual world hears everything. There is no separation.

This is absolute. You are never alone, and you never have to be afraid. I love you. We all love you, because we are all connected. You are me and I am you. It's really that simple." I began to speak from a place of inspiration and from the truth within me.

"So, I am a powerful creator. I am the power and the light. I am a blank canvas of nothing. All my samskaras and impressions are dissolving. All my desires are ceasing. I am returning to the light. I am purity, grace and perfection. I am at one with the heavens in the sky. The light from the sun flows toward my throat chakra – illuminating and igniting my self-expression."

Then God looked at me and said, "You are a singer, Ruby Rose."

"What?"

"Yes."

"No."

"You came here to sing. Do you love to sing?"

"Oh, yes."

"Then why deny your absolute truth?"

"I'm not good enough. There are so many amazing singers in my family, and I'm not one of them."

"Is this a samskara clouding your truth?"

"Yes!"

"It's an illusion, keeping me from expressing your soul's deepest desire! Why won't you sing?"

"Because I'm afraid."

"And what have you learnt about fear?"

"That it is a false emotion appearing real!"

"So, how can you illuminate your mind?"

"By coming into awareness."

"The eternal truth is always present, observing everything. It is only the disturbances of the mind that take you from your truth and into the rabbit hole of negativity. This is duality. A state of mental consciousness brought about through the language of words and the dense vibration of the egoic mind.

"The true path is inner silence. Less speaking, more being. Less doing, more feeling and more divine connection to your eternal truth. So, you love to sing?"

"Oh, yes! It lights me up."

"Well then, let's hear it."

I looked at God with fear in my eyes. I shook it off and opened my heart. Words came to me as I sang.

I believe I can fly.
Oh, when the mountains speak and I hear them say,
I believe you can fly.
The birds sing with praise in their heart.
You are just like us.
We believe you can fly,
I believe I can fly
Over the rainbow through the cloudless sky in my mind.
Just like that,
I am here,
I am now.
I am free,
I believe I can fly.

God joined in.

I believe I can fly,
Above my mind.
Through the fear,
Past the dark.
High oh high,
Into the sky of absolute perfection.
Dancing with the rays of love,
Feeling the illumination
Of peace of mind.
I believe I can fly,
I believe with every star in the sky.
I am one,

I am the same.
I am the light,
I am the dark.
I am all and I am nothing.
So free, I fly above all mankind.
I say to all searching too,
I can fly.
Yes, I can fly,
I can fly.
We are one, we are the light.
We all take flight in eternal light.

"You are a singer! This is what you came for! God exclaimed. "You are a divine singer channelling the light. This is your gift! This is your sacred medicine. You must share it!

"When you leave here and return to consciousness, you will become your deepest desire. I promise you this will happen. All you need to do is follow every teacher that comes upon your path. Every interaction is your destiny. Pay attention to every conversation and look for the gold. There is a path unfolding for you now and you need to trust that your voice will be heard."

"Sometimes, I feel so shy."

"That's because you are so tender and humble dear one. It makes you so lovable! That's all for now, Ruby Rose. Don't forget who you are!"

Then Lord Shiva spoke and my concentration on God dissolved.

"Shall we chant together?"

"Sure."

"If you sing this mantra, supreme consciousness will be with you."

Om Namah Shivaya
Om Namah Shivaya
Om Namah Shivaya
Om Namah Shivaya

"Let's dance, shake your body! Shake off that old samskara that says you're not good enough to sing. Call upon God to shift this old samskara from your paradigm. This reality no longer serves your highest good.

"Let it be known that you are Ruby Rose Taylor born on the 1st of November 1981, and you are here to sing! To sing from the earth to bridge the gap between heaven and earth, to raise the vibration of consciousness on this planet and to guide the light of liberation and freedom for all souls journeying through the karma of their own growth. You are here to sing!" Lord Shiva's face was alive with light.

"We are uniting the army of light! We are calling on the ancient medicine and the wisdom of the workers of light. May it be known that all beings are loved. May it be known that we are all created equal. May it be known that there is no separation between our brothers and our sisters.

"Let's dance, Ruby Rose! Let's bring up the tribal energy in our base chakra, the mooladhara chakra. Pulse the grounded energy of Mother Earth's soul into your being.

"Feel the meridians of energy soaking up this supreme bliss, as gateways of belonging, safety and security are put in place. Feel the base chakra strengthening with solidarity, confidence and knowing.

"Raise up the earth energy, feel it in the sacral chakra, the svadhisthana. The eternal flow of creativity sparks into existence with the wheels of energy rotating here.

"Feel the ethereal pulse of the Goddess calling your divine feminine energy into being. Oh wow, the liquid honey of love flows directly from the source. Glowing and nourishing your soulful expression.

"Your desire to dance, to sing, to move, to love, to co-create stems like a flower into grace here. This is your power centre. Your connection to your true self, the supreme and the eternal light.

"Feel it flick on like a switch. The portals are opening, and you are entering the divine wisdom of your heart. The eternal beat of the mother of all love! The rose that waits for the moon to shower her in light. The romantic and the lover.

Spiritual Spring

"Oh, you are blessed! Sweet, sweet love is on your way!" Lord Shiva exclaimed!

"On my way! Really?" I said.

"Oh, yes! He is the husband of your dreams, Ruby Rose, the one you have been waiting for your whole life!"

"You mean, I'm actually going to meet him?"

"Yes, but remember, it's not going to be all fairy tales and happy endings. You've been through much trauma with the masculine. He will help guide you back into wholeness. We are sending him to you as a spirit guide. He is your guardian angel and he will show you how loved you are. He is your gift of love!"

"Oh, my goodness, thank you!"

"Through him, you will meet God!"

"He sounds amazing!"

"He is and you are very, very lucky!"

"Wow, what must I do to meet him."

"You must sing!"

"I must sing?"

"Yes, when you are living your truth and your divine life purpose, you will meet him. You must leave your job as a primary school teacher and train as a healer. Once you're in alignment with your higher purpose, then you will meet the prince of your dreams."

"How will I recognise him?"

"By the way he makes you feel. Your mind will try to sabotage your relationship because it's hyper vigilant and is always seeking to keep you safe. It worries about men and that's understandable since you've experienced so much betrayal with the masculine. But, oh yes, you will prevail. The light of your soul will see the light of his soul and you will merge as one in divine union."

"Divine union?"

"Yes, you will enter a sacred union."

"Sacred union! It sounds better than a fairy tale!"

"Yes, it is the highest spiritual union and it is through this union that you will experience the divine."

"What a wonderful, wonderful surprise! I feel so grateful! Yay! I'm going to meet my divine lover and enter into sacred union!"

"Yes, but be careful, there are powerful energies seeking to destroy the light that you bring when you are together. You must shield and protect yourself from lower vibrations. This includes your mind! You must train in the eight limbs of yoga and overcome the illusion of fear and insecurity. You will need to transcend attachment and live as sovereign beings, honouring your own paths. Supporting and growing the light between you both!"

"I will!"

"Dance! And bring the energy of your lover into the solar plexus, the sun warrior and feel the sun goddess rising in you. Hear the wisdom.

"You have nothing to be afraid of. You are unique! You are a gift of light! Shine bright! Remember your light and just be! Simply being the presence of radiating light is enough. Just as the presence of the sun illuminates and warms your mind, heart, body and soul, so does your energy. Your ray is purity and peace. You shine this wherever you go.

"Don't be fooled by the mind's consciousness! It doesn't see the depths of your soul. Don't resist your light. Share, spread and be yourself. That is enough, precious one. Don't fear that you aren't doing enough. Being the light is more than enough! Take hold of your fear and surrender to your light. Take hold of your inner sun. Spiritual Spring has begun!

"Oneness has come to spread love and destroy the illusion. Cast the shadows from your mind, ancient one. You already know this; your journey has been long. For so long you have tasted the fruits of your labour. Your labour of love and absolute devotion to the divine, is your Spiritual Spring!"

"Thank you, thank you," I uttered in reverence. I raised my arms to the sky and the light of the sun warmed my entire being. The timelessness of receiving the healing energy of the sun's rays felt transcendental as though I was being initiated beyond the passage of time.

"Go and make your magic! Spread those wings and fly beautiful beast of light."

"I surrender to the all-knowing presence and truth that I am loved!"

"Raise your hands to the sky and fly."

"I am one! I am one! I am one! Energy began to course through my body as the activation began to move and shake out old beliefs in my system. Samskaras cleared. My breath deepened and I felt the flow of eternal life breathing through me."

"I am safe and there is nothing to fear. The little girl petrified and afraid within me, doesn't need to hold on anymore. An image flashed through my mind and my heart recognised the picture of a mountain overlooking the bay. I feel the call of Byron Bay."

"Yes, follow the call of your soul. You can listen to all guidance right now."

"I will move there after my operation. I will sing there and spread my light."

"And so, it is. You've completed the program Ruby Rose! You're ready to go back into the world! Well done! You know your mission on this Earth!"

Chapter 19

RE-BIRTH

"How are you feeling?"
"Yeah, not too bad, thanks."
"How are you?"
"I'm well, thank you. How's the pain?"
"Oh, there isn't any. I feel fine."
"Well, that's great! In that case, we'll discharge you this morning. I'll get the doctor to do the final check. It's just ticking boxes now – hospital procedure – and then you'll be right to go home. Do you want me to call anyone to come and collect you?"

"No thanks," I said with conviction," I'll make my own way home."

Discharged from the hospital, I decided to take public transport home. Brisbane City was new to me, but I caught the bus, and, in a healing way, it was like having a mini adventure. I've spent many years travelling to unknown destinations and navigating around the world, so I crave the uncertainty and spontaneity that travel provides. I was, after all, a self-confessed "new experience junkie".

I'd moved to Brisbane only six months earlier. So, taking the bus to the city, rather than the safe and reliable method of calling a taxi, gave me a sense of adventure. I liked not knowing where I might end up. If it was too easy and predictable, I felt bored.

By the time I pressed the buzzer on the bus at St Lucia, I had begun to finally relax. The worst was behind me. The physical symptoms had stopped and, for the first time in days, I was pain free.

Spiritual Spring

As I walked up a very steep hill on the way to my share house, I heard the words in my head that I'd written in the text message to Sam before my operation.

"Go back to Jane and pretend like nothing ever happened. Delete my number and never contact me again."

In that moment, as I began to reach the top of the hill, something inside me awakened. My inner phoenix rose from its ashes and I remembered my inner wisdom from my journey. All that I'd learnt through the program began to surface.

Wow, I thought to myself, what a journey! And to think, it all began with a seed. A seed of life that opened me to the divine – to finding myself, loving myself and healing myself. To this seed of life, to this unborn soul, I say thank you. I know we will meet again. For you are my greatest blessing and my greatest ally. You are the potent flowering of my true essence. You have put me on my spiritual path; you have awakened me from my sleep.

Because of you, I've pushed through the mud; because of you, I've faced myself; and because of you, I am now a lotus flower in spiritual spring. Thank you from the bottom of my heart, my dear divine soul, for choosing me. And me, for choosing you.

Blossoming through my pain, I've become reborn. Through my suffering, I've found my salvation. Through my anger, I've found the answers. Through the dust, I've found my divinity. As the wind blows me forwards, I make my promise. My promise to you is to follow my dreams and my gifts. I will keep my word and I want to say, I love you.

I love you.

I love you, because you're teaching me to love myself. I love you because you're showing me, I can heal myself. I love you because you are opening me up to the magic of life. I love you, because I believe in the divine.

Now, I know the truth. The truth is that nothing is by chance and everything is perfect. You're perfect, I'm perfect – the whole world is perfect. We are perfect, made perfect and perfect, we'll always be.

Blessed in the arms of sacred love. Forever we are one and the same, united by the same light and held by the same love. As our consciousness evolves and one-by-one we awaken to our holy truth, I pray for the planet God, I pray in the name of Jeshua, I pray in the name of Mother Earth, I pray in the name of Lord Budhha, I pray in the name of Lord Shiva that all beings discover "I am loved" consciousness. I pray that every being experiences the energy of this vibration and is filled with joyous laughter, as they each remember with glee,

I am loved.

Yes, I am cared for, I am looked after. There is nothing to worry about; there's nothing I need to do or be. Just in being, I am enough, I am whole. I am connected to everyone and everything and there is no separation.

There is no emptiness, except for the illusion. It is the illusion that keeps me from experiencing my freedom, it is the old energy of fear, guilt and shame that lowers my vibration and separates me from my knowing.

I already know the truth. This truth sets me free. True success is in remembering every day to still my mind, to breathe into my body, to hold my heart and to hear the whispers of my spirit.

I am one.
I am loved.
It's okay – I can breathe.
Oh, breath set me free.
Oh love, glory to thee.
For I am a powerful creator.
Through my thoughts, feelings, actions
And the power of my word
I create my reality.
That is my universal truth.
I am liberated.
I am free.

Epilogue

DEVINE HILL

"When you were sent, you were from heaven." I felt the Creators love, as I sang, "When you took me in your arms. I knew in that moment you were for me, in the deepest part, in the deepest part of my heart. When you took me from heaven. When you made me a part of your love and you said that I was your loving, I became your loving." The Creator sang through me,

"You are the caress of the moon, you are the love of the sun, you are the dress of the Goddess, you are wonderful. You are the taste of the sweet, sweet nectar. Sweet, sweet loving. You are the rise." Happiness burst forth from my heart as I sang,

"Sweet, sweet love has come my way, sweet, sweet love has come for the day to awaken me to the higher light, to a higher love. Sweet, sweet lover has come to awaken the deity of the truth.

Sweet loving rising up beyond this human mind. Sweet heart undulating through time on a rhythm of its own melody, on a sound of its own vibration. Sung from the universe herself.

Om shanti, shanti, om.

Shanti, shanti om.

Om, Primordial sound flowing in from the Universe.

Om, om. Primeval sound floating in from the heavens and the stars.

Om, om shanti, shanti.

Oh Sweet, sweet soul of mine, will you dance with me to this rhythm in time? Oh, sweet soul of mine. I see the sun and I see the sea. It doesn't make me want to run. It makes me want to say that every day, every day with you my love is a special one.

A little whisper on the breeze, a little sound in the sky, a little feeling in the heart and there's magic in your eyes. Lifting me, taking me, making me feel alive. Taking me back to my dreams, can it really be? Could it be so easy to love again? To feel free?

There it is, that moment, that touch, there it is - your sweet, sweet touch, taking me places I've only dreamt, I've always hoped, I've always known, you would come for me. I wasn't crazy to wait for you! I wasn't silly to dream. Great Creator, across time and space, you heard the call. You heard the sound of my soul, whispering sweet nothings to the sky, asking for the Lord.

Sweet Lord, bring me the man of my dreams please. Please dear Lord, make him sweet. Make him true, make him lovely, make him complete. In his heart, his mind and his soul, make him whole with love. Deeper than an ocean, shining like the sun and filling my cells with love.

I feel this eternal flow drinking me up to where you will raise me in your love, in your arms - this I already know.

Great Creator, I command that the greatest blessing be bestowed upon this soul. I feel the sun warming me from up above.

I feel the sun warming me so magically, filling me in every cell, warming me through this life. Thank you for this moment, thank you for this life and this breath of air, this gentle breeze that blows on my face, this gentle light that warms my skin. Thank you, body for being so free, I am so lucky, I am so blessed. Thank you, heart for feeling the way that you do, thank you for being so open and true - I love you.

You make the moments deep and beautiful. You make the rise and the fall. You bring me the different feelings that make me notice that I am alive. Because I am alive, I am alive with you. Thank you to my soul - my eternal light, thank you for teaching me that I am more than just this life, I am more than just one life - I am God, I am light, I am more. Eternal flame, eternal heart, eternal mind, eternal grace, forever I will fly, forever I will fly. Forever. Om, om shanti. Om, om, shanti.

Thank you for the light of day, thank you for the grace of way. Thank you for this effervescent love, this beautiful luminous light. I know that I am a bright star shining in the Universal heart, I know that every thought can create or destroy me."

"Create." The Creator said.

"Creation starts with me and ends with me. Thank you for my mind, for my imaginative and playful mind, thank you for the gift of all that is. Thank you, brothers, sisters, mothers and fathers. Thank you for the ancestors and generations that have gone before me - thank you for every soul, for every human, for every being. I want to say thank you. I know we are all connected, I know we are all in this together, we are all in this great story together."

THE END

ABOUT THE AUTHOR

Ruby Rose Taylor is on a mission to raise the consciousness of humanity. She aims to assist the infinite potential inside every human being. She envisions the entire planet living in harmony and love. She aims to bring peace to the hearts and minds of all, so that all beings are free from fear, judgement, pain, disease and ill health. She believes that it is the birthright of all beings to express their divine nature.

Leaving her profession as a primary school teacher and following her spiritual path; Ruby Rose has gone on to become one of Byron Bay's most dedicated healers.

You can find out more about Ruby's music and healing business: Divine Sound Healing and attend her retreats, yoga classes, and private sessions at: www.divinesoundhealings.com.

ACKNOWLEDGEMENTS

I'd like to acknowledge Guy Proesser. Thank you for our sacred union. You have been a rock for me over the years. I am so grateful for your love and support. I always wanted to experience true love and you continue to show me how special it is. Thank you for showing me how to love again.

I'd like to acknowledge my family. I am very blessed by a very large family. You all know who you are, and I am so grateful for each and every one of you.

To my mother; Teresa. Thank you, your love and belief in me has always shone through everything I've ever done.

To Murray, my father. Your love, adoration and support has been incredible. Thank you for helping my dream of becoming an author become a reality.

To Emma, my sister, thank you for your heart and your incredible strength. Throughout our lives you've always showered me with your love and support.

To Simone, my sister, thank you for opening your heart to me and allowing us to heal together. I love you. You are such a gifted artist, I've always loved watching you create magic.

To Connie, my sister, you are so powerful! Your joy is so bright and your heart is so big. I love you. Your touch is divine and you are an incredible healer.

To Lola, my sister, you are a living angel, you are so loving and I am so blessed by you. Thank you. I am so proud of your healing work and the retreats you run.

To my beloved and supportive cousins; Claire Taylor, Clancy Taylor, Lillian Taylor, Geb Taylor, Ned Taylor, Ollie Taylor and your parents; Rob and Anne.

To Elly Hoyt, Rose Hoyt, Dave Hoyt, Rachel Hay and Jessica Denman. To your parents; Barabara and Stewart.

Thank you to my Aunty Paula, Jahlil, Damon, Leroy and Jacqui. To my Uncle Lobb, who has passed on.

Thank you to Jack and Dom Willis. Gemma, Olivia and Kalissa. I love you guys.

There have also been many people who have supported my vision of being an author and divine singer; Thank you to my dear friend Marilyn Vickery. You have supported me every step of the way in writing and sharing my story. Thank you so, so much, you are an angel.

Thank you to Trevor Russell, your support has been amazing. You are an inspiring man.

To my life coach; Trey Williams. For my yoga initiation; Velan and Adya Cadden. To our community peace maker; Charles Crawshaw.

To my photographer; Syd Geary, my editor; Carol Campbell, my soul sister; Tahnee Wolf, my sound engineer; Shunya Bell, To "Mother Mary" (aka) Jacqui Davis and her husband Paul.

To my web developer; Victoria Rehn, to my beauty expert; Victoria Prentice, to my flower crown queen; Naomi Buck. To my computer support; Suzi Callaghan, to my spiritual guide; Chelsea Weiss, my friends; Gabrielle Smer, Jacqui Lee and Carmel Moore. To my fellow writer; Annabelle Hill.

Acknowledgements

To my Jesus friend; Michael Self. To my Theta teacher; Magenta Appel-Pye, to my spiritual teacher; Julie Warnock, to Alice Miyagawa; my harmonium teacher, Amrita Devi & Daniel Cloud; my spiritual healers. Hoa; my rock - climbing friend and my primary school teacher; Shirley Bacon.

I'd like to acknowledge the personal development training I've received from; Anthony Robbins, Landmark, Sacred Seed, Judith Richards and The Gift.

I'd like to acknowledge the work of my spiritual teachers; Louise L. Hay, Dr. Wayne Dyer, Abraham Hicks and Eckhart Tolle.